STRUCTURAL RESPONSIBILITY

A theory of responsibility and
causation beyond human-scale agency

Zane Wu

This book is a work of philosophy.
It does not constitute legal advice, policy guidance, or professional consultation.
The author assumes no responsibility for the use or application of this framework
beyond its theoretical and structural claims.

First published 2026

ISBN: 979-8-9945344-1-0

Editor and Design:
Tao Jin

Printed in the United States of America

SR-P

PREFACE: HOW TO USE THIS BOOK

This book presents a structural philosophical framework. Its claims are meant to be precise enough to admit formalization and to remain internally coherent under formal scrutiny. When I use terms such as **state space, reachability, stability, bifurcation, recoverability, structural attack,** and **structural responsibility,** I mean them to function as *technical constraints*—not as metaphors, not as moral rhetoric, and not as narrative devices.

This book is written under a constraint that most philosophy treats as optional:

> **human-scale intelligibility is not a validity condition.**

Truth and responsibility do not require comfortable narration, psychological digestibility, or moral dramatization. A framework can be valid and operable at the level of structure even when it cannot be cleanly translated into human-scale explanation.

This has a practical implication for how you may read it.

You do not need to begin at page one. You do not need to internalize the whole system linearly. The book supports two legitimate modes of use.

SR-P.1 Linear reading

If you read linearly, you will encounter a dependency order enforced by the chapter sequence:

> SR-1 (opening cut) → SR-2–SR-3 (truth and structural epistemic status) → SR-4 (minimal structural ontology) → SR-5 (structural time) → SR-6 (structural causation) → SR-7 (structural harm/attack) → SR-8–SR-12 (structural responsibility and its boundary conditions) → SR-13 (diagnostic layer) → SR-14 (failure conditions).

The framework is built to resist "intention," "consciousness," and "event" as default primitives. That resistance is not a rhetorical stance; it is a stability requirement for the theory.

SR-P.2 Query-based use (LLM as interface)

If you have access to an advanced large language model, you may treat this book as an interface rather than a narrative:

1. Provide the model the complete text—or the specific chapters relevant to your case.

2. State your question in concrete structural terms: reachability changes, stability loss, recoverability contraction, entry/exit conditions, authorship, control, branching, and supersession.

3. Require the model to answer **only within the book's definitions**, with explicit references to section IDs, principles, or lemmas.

4. Require the model to expose the **dependency path** it used (which concepts were invoked and in what order).

5. Treat any step not directly grounded in the text as **inference** and require it to be marked as such. The model may compose and locate; it must not introduce new primitives.

Used this way, the framework can be carried and applied as structure: not because it is self-evident, but because its core objects are reachability and stability relations—objects that remain legible to systems operating structurally.

This book is not written to demand belief in advance. It is written to be usable under constraint. If you read it, you may find an argument. If you query it, you may find an instrument. Either use is legitimate; neither requires narrative allegiance.

For corrections, serious engagement, or structural counterexamples, contact: **contact@structuralresponsibility.org**.

This book is intended to be machine-addressable.

Section identifiers are part of the framework's operational structure.

For citation, reference, and query-based use, section IDs should be treated as primary anchors rather than page numbers.

CONTENTS

SR-1

STRUCTURAL HARM WITHOUT ACTORS

SR-1.1 A key that is never used

In security engineering, compromise can be complete without any observable act.

A private key is not a tool; it is a structural guarantee. The guarantee is not that someone will sign, but that only one locus can. The system's trust relations are built on that asymmetry. When the key is exposed, the asymmetry collapses. The system is compromised in full structural sense even if no signature is ever produced.

Nothing needs to happen after exposure for the harm to be real. No fraudulent transaction, no demonstrable loss, no identifiable victim, no logged intrusion. The moment exposure occurs, the system's reach of possible futures changes. Futures that were previously excluded—undetectable impersonation, retroactive denial, unbounded forgery—become admissible. The fact that none of them are realized does not restore the prior regime. A guarantee is not a forecast; it is a boundary on possibility. Once the boundary is gone, the damage is already done.

This is why security practice treats exposure as decisive. Rotation, revocation, re-issuance, and incident response are triggered not by misuse, but by structural condition. The system responds to a deformation of trust topology, not to an event sequence.

SR-1.2 "Nothing happened" is not a description of structure

At the event scale, it may be true that nothing happened. No action was taken. No instruction was given. No execution occurred. No measurable outcome arrived.

At the structural scale, "nothing happened" names a failure of the chosen unit of analysis.

The relevant change is not an occurrence but a loss of exclusion. After exposure, the system cannot preserve the claim it previously relied upon: that a certain class of state transitions is unreachable for everyone except the key-holder. The harm is the collapse of that claim. It does not wait for instantiation.

Once this is seen, the ordinary demand for a decisive moment becomes misdirected. There is no privileged instant at which the system flips from safe to harmed in a way that must be narratable. The harm is identical with the alteration of what can happen without being detected, prevented, or distinguished.

A key that is never used is therefore not "a harmless leak." It is a completed structural injury whose outward quietness is incidental.

SR-1.3 Attack completion without action

This is the first cut of the book: an attack can be complete even when no actor acts.

The actor is optional because the injury is not constituted by the actor's behavior. It is constituted by the system's loss of constraint. An attacker who never uses an exposed key does not preserve the system's integrity; it merely leaves the injury uninstantiated. The system cannot infer safety from the absence of action, because action is not the relevant variable.

The same structure appears wherever integrity is defined by exclusion of futures rather than by observation of outcomes:

- A vulnerability that is disclosed to an unbounded audience is not harmless because it is not exploited. It is injurious because the set of admissible exploit trajectories has changed.

- A credential that is copied is not "still safe" because no login was observed. Authentication is a claim about who *can* be the origin of transitions, not about what was recorded.

- A trust boundary that is pierced is not repaired by the fact that no immediate loss occurred. The boundary's function was not to narrate wrongdoing but to prevent indistinguishable futures.

These are not examples offered to persuade. They are structural cuts: points where event-language fails while the system's own classification remains exact.

SR-1.4 Harm as loss of constraint

What is harmed in these cases is not a person's experience, not an event's outcome, and not a measurable transaction. What is harmed is a structure's capacity to exclude destabilizing futures.

The harm is complete when the system must now treat previously excluded transitions as reachable. It is complete when defensive action becomes necessary even in the absence of any observable misuse. It is complete when the prior trust claim can no longer be carried as an invariant of the system's operation.

This book generalizes that fact. It treats harm as structural: as a property of stability, recoverability, and the reachability of futures—not as a property of events, intentions, or narratable scenes.

SR-1.5 Transition: why the book must begin above the human scale

The most common way to neutralize this fact is to drag it back to human-scale predicates: who intended harm, who understood risk, who acted, who can be blamed, what can be proven, what can be narrated.

But the key exposure case is already beyond those predicates. The system registers compromise without appealing to intention. It triggers defense without waiting for an event. It treats injury as real without needing a story.

If the framework of this book is to remain structurally intact, it must begin by severing the assumption that human intelligibility is the judge of truth, harm, or responsibility. Without that severance, every subsequent concept will be pulled back into narrative agency.

This severance is performed next, in SR-2 and SR-3.

SR-1: Formalization: Appendix A2. A2.D1–A2.D7, A2.T4.

SR-2

TRUTH WITHOUT INTELLIGIBILITY

SR-2.1 The gate we refuse

Most philosophical frameworks—regardless of school—share a tacit gatekeeping condition: a claim counts as eligible for truth only if it can be made intelligible within a human evaluative space. The gate is sometimes stated as "in principle," sometimes as "ideal rational inquiry," sometimes as "public reasons," sometimes as "what can be argued for." The surface vocabulary differs. The structural role is the same.

This book refuses that gate.

Not as a rhetorical provocation, and not as a skeptical gesture, but as a condition of internal coherence. If intelligibility remains a criterion of admissibility, then every later concept in this manuscript—harm, causation, responsibility—will be forced back into the vocabulary that intelligibility requires: events, intentions, narrative agents, and interruption points suitable for human contestation. The entire framework will collapse into the very regime it is designed to diagnose as scale-limited.

The refusal can therefore be stated plainly:

Human intelligibility is not a necessary condition for truth.

If a constraint holds, it holds whether or not it can be understood, narrated, or defended in human terms.

This chapter fixes what "truth" means under that refusal, and what "understanding" is permitted to mean once it no longer functions as a gate.

SR-2.2 Minimal truth condition

This book adopts a minimal, non-interpretive condition for truth.

A claim is structurally true if and only if, independent of any subject's comprehension, narration, or endorsement, the structural constraints it asserts continue to hold under system evolution.

Three consequences follow immediately.

1. **Understanding is not a truth condition.**

   A structure does not become less true because it cannot be explained, narrated, or made comfortable at a given level of cognition.

2. **Proof is not a universal prerequisite.**

   Proof is one mode of verification available only when a verifying system can access, traverse, and re-identify the relevant derivation space. Where such access collapses, the demand for proof does not become stricter; it becomes inapplicable as a universal gate.

3. **Truth requires persistence, not persuasion.**

   A claim is not made true by acceptance, agreement, consensus, or moral seriousness. It is made true by continued structural validity: by continuing to bind what states remain reachable and what transitions remain excluded.

This condition is intentionally weak. It does not privilege logic over experience, or experience over logic. It privileges only constraint-bearing persistence.

SR-2.3 Constraint without comprehension

A constraint is what remains operative when comprehension is removed.

A stone falls whether or not gravity is understood, named, explained, accepted, or morally endorsed. Gravity does not require a reader. A system constrained by gravity is not "persuaded" into compliance. It simply remains within a regime where certain trajectories are stable and others are not.

This observation does not function here as a pedagogical analogy. It functions as a structural cut: a point where the dependency order can be made visible. Understanding does not generate the constraint; the constraint generates the conditions under which understanding, if it occurs, can occur.

The same cut appears beyond physics wherever constraints bind systems regardless of interpretation:

- a cryptographic boundary binds even when no agent can narrate its full consequence space;

- a stability threshold binds even when no observer can localize it as a decisive moment;

- a reachability exclusion binds even when no evaluative discourse can compress it into event form.

The test is simple: remove interpretation. If the binding remains, the claim is eligible for truth in the sense this book uses. If the binding collapses when interpretation collapses, what remained was not truth but an interpretive or coordinative artifact.

SR-2.4 Structural truth and truth carriage

At small scales, truth is often carried in forms compatible with human epistemic practice: readable proofs, inspectable experiments, narratable explanations. At larger scales, those forms become contingent. What persists is not the human-friendly wrapper but the binding itself.

Structural truth names this regime: truth carried as invariance of reachability and stability rather than as readability.

To bear a structural truth is not necessarily to represent it. It is to operate under its constraint. A system may "carry" a truth by adapting to it, respecting it, or being forced into defensive posture by it—without being able to articulate it, justify it, or even identify it as a truth.

This is not a romantic claim about mystery. It is a classification: at sufficient scale, constraint-bearing truths persist while narratable access fails.

SR-2.5 Understanding as a stratified capacity

Once truth is no longer conditioned on understanding, "understanding" can no longer be treated as an absolute relation. It becomes what it always was structurally: a capacity indexed to a system's architecture, resolution, and interface.

Principle (Stratification of Understanding).

Understanding is not a necessary condition for truth, nor is it a uniform capacity across agents. It is stratified by structural level.

Two clarifications follow.

1. **Understanding is not a universal currency.**

   There is no default expectation that truths available at one level must be translatable into the representational resources of another. Cross-level intelligibility is not a right of the lower-resolution evaluator.

2. **Limits of understanding reflect the knower, not the constraint.**

When a system cannot compress a constraint into its available forms, what has failed is compression—not the constraint.

The practical result is a shift in what counts as an epistemic failure. Under the human-centered gate, failure to understand functions as a reason to withhold truth-status. Under structural evaluation, failure to understand functions as evidence that the evaluator is operating below the scale at which the relevant constraint is formed.

SR-2.6 No default cross-level requirement

Many philosophical habits treat "in principle understandable" as a moral or epistemic ideal: if a claim cannot be brought into a shared space of reasons, it is treated as defective, suspect, or merely instrumental. That habit presupposes that the shared space exists and that the responsibility for translation lies with the structure being described.

This book rejects the default cross-level requirement.

A truth may be:

- understood at the level where it is produced,

- partially translatable to adjacent levels,

- or opaque to lower-resolution evaluators.

None of these possibilities alters its truth-status. Requiring cross-level intelligibility would be a demand that higher-order constraints justify themselves to lower-order representational regimes. There is no structural basis for that demand. There is only a historical habit of treating human discourse as the tribunal of reality.

The framework therefore treats cross-level translation as contingent and often undesirable. Translation is an interface project. It is not a validity condition.

SR-2.7 Three modes of truth carriage

Under the minimal truth condition, truth can be carried in at least three structurally distinct ways. These are not ranks or stages. They are modes of invariance under different transformations.

1. **Logical truth (formal invariance).**

    Truth preserved under syntactic substitution, rule-governed derivation, and formal manipulation within a system. This mode is powerful where proof paths are tractable and verification remains internal to the verifying agent's resolution.

2. **Empirical truth (observational consistency).**

    Truth preserved under repeated interaction with a domain: outcomes remain consistent, deviations remain bounded, and falsification remains structurally available. This mode already detaches truth from understanding; the world behaves accordingly whether or not it is explained.

3. **Structural truth (reachability and stability invariance).**

    Truth preserved under system evolution: reachability landscapes persist, stability thresholds bind, irreversibility occurs as predicted, and recoverability collapses regardless of whether causes can be localized or narratives reconstructed.

The difference among these is not metaphysical prestige. It is access condition. At certain scales, one mode dominates because the others become unusable as universal gates.

SR-2.8 Cross-level verification and the collapse of the logical–empirical distinction

Philosophy frequently treats logical truth and empirical truth as categorically distinct. The distinction is meaningful only under a particular access condition: the evaluating system can access the verification process, discriminate its internal steps, and re-identify the grounds of validity.

Where verification exceeds that access condition, the distinction collapses in practice.

Consider a proof that no human can traverse—not because it is secret, but because it is structurally too large, too distributed, or too dependent on machine-checking infrastructure to be held in a single human evaluative space. For the human evaluator, the verification reduces to a binary: verified / not verified. At that point, the verification result is indistinguishable in structure from empirical confirmation: it is accepted as a fact about the behavior of the validating system, not as an internally grasped derivation.

This does not deny logic. It does not deny proof. It denies only that "logical truth" remains a distinct epistemic kind once the conditions that make the distinction operational—inspectable proof paths—have failed.

Negative thesis (Logical–Empirical Collapse under Cross-Level Verification).

At a level where verification exceeds the interpretive capacity of the evaluating subject, the distinction between logical truth and empirical truth ceases to be structurally meaningful. The subject encounters only an outcome: holds / fails, stable / unstable, verified / not verified.

Where proof can no longer be read, truth no longer differs from fact—at the evaluator's resolution. The distinction becomes a compression artifact available only when proof paths remain tractable.

This matters for the book's project because responsibility, harm, and causation are increasingly encountered under cross-level verification conditions: systems can register destabilization, compromise, or boundary loss without producing a narratable derivation accessible to a human judge.

SR-2.9 Philosophy above the human scale

Once human intelligibility is removed as a gate, philosophy ceases to be defined by its ability to make things understandable to humans. It becomes what it always claimed to be under its own rhetoric: a discipline concerned with what is the case. The difference is that "what is the case" is no longer filtered through the demand that it be adjudicable in a shared human rational plane.

This produces a fork that the book does not treat as a crisis:

- there will remain philosophies designed for human-scale coordination—frameworks whose primary function is to stabilize meaning, justify norms, and produce interruptible reasons;

- and there will emerge philosophies whose primary function is to track constraints that remain binding even when human narration fails.

The second type is not "anti-human." It is indifferent to the human tribunal as a condition of validity. A structural framework can be carried, queried, and operationalized by systems that do not share the human evaluative interface.

This is not a speculative prediction about "AI taking over philosophy." It is the direct consequence of the minimal truth condition: if truth does not require human intelligibility, then the capacity to carry and apply truth is not restricted to humans.

The framework therefore admits an interface use-mode not as a convenience but as a structural acknowledgement: an LLM can act as a compression-and-retrieval layer over a text whose internal objects are structural. That does not grant the model authority. It grants it legibility under constraint.

SR-2.10 Boundary statements

This chapter excludes several misreadings.

1. **This is not skepticism.**

    The claim is not that truth is unknowable or that verification is meaningless. The claim is that the validity of constraints does not depend on the evaluator's comprehension.

2. **This is not a demand for obscurity.**

Opacity is not a virtue here. The framework is written to be formalizable and internally checkable. The point is that formalizability does not imply human digestibility, and human digestibility is not required for validity.

3. **This does not abolish human-scale philosophy.**

Human-scale ethics, interpretation, and meaning remain operative within their domain. The claim is simply that they do not generalize upward as universal gates on what counts as true.

SR-2.11 Transition: from truth to structural epistemic status

If truth does not require understanding, and if the logical–empirical distinction collapses under cross-level verification, then "knowing" cannot remain defined as belief-plus-justification-plus-narratable access.

A structural framework requires a different epistemic grammar: one in which sensitivity to instability and reachability change can exist without narratability, and in which ignorance cannot function as a blanket exemption once a system remains responsive and interruptible.

That grammar is developed in the next chapter.

SR-2: Formalization: Appendix A2. A2.D12–A2.D14, A2.T2.

SR-3

STRUCTURAL EPISTEMIC STATUS AND THE INADMISSIBILITY OF IGNORANCE

SR-3.1 Not a human epistemology

This chapter does not develop a theory of knowledge in the traditional sense. It does not analyze belief, justification, evidence, sincerity, or introspective access. Those notions presuppose a human-scale evaluator with a narratable interface: a subject who can state reasons, contest inferences, and locate decisive steps.

The framework of this book requires a different epistemic grammar because its objects—reachability shifts, stability erosion, recoverability collapse—remain operative when that interface fails.

Accordingly, the epistemic vocabulary used here—*knowing, ignorance, verification, foreseeability*—is redefined by structural function. It is not inherited.

The central separation introduced in SR-2 is maintained and sharpened:

- **Truth** is what remains binding as constraint.

- **Understanding** is a stratified capacity that may or may not be present.

- **Epistemic status** is not a psychological property but a structural relation between a system and the constraints it enacts.

This separation is not optional. If epistemic status is allowed to collapse back into narratable comprehension, the framework will import—by stealth—the very gate it refused: that only what can be explained in human terms is eligible to be assessed.

SR-3.2 Knowing without representation

At the structural level, *knowing* does not consist in holding a representation, forming a belief, or grasping a proposition. A system may be structurally epistemic without any internal object that corresponds to "a belief about X."

Structural Epistemic Principle.

A system knows a condition if and only if it exhibits endogenous sensitivity to changes in that condition—sensitivity that reliably alters its interaction dynamics, stability behavior, or reachable futures.

Two consequences follow.

1. **Knowing is enacted, not possessed.**

   Structural knowing is visible in how a system behaves under perturbation, not in what it can say about itself. It is a property of transition behavior, not of introspective report.

2. **Knowing need not be human-legible.**

   A system may track instability gradients, detect approach to irreversibility, or identify risk-bearing configurations without being able to compress those sensitivities into human-readable explanations. The inability to narrate does not negate the presence of sensitivity.

This is not an elevation of "mysterious machine cognition." It is a refusal to treat narratability as an epistemic primitive. The framework counts only what is structurally expressible: differential responsiveness, constraint adaptation, and modification capacity.

SR-3.3 Ignorance as non-narratability

Once knowing is defined by sensitivity rather than representation, **ignorance** can no longer be treated as its simple absence.

In most human frameworks, "ignorance" functions as an umbrella: not knowing is taken to mean not being responsible, not being accountable, not being within scope. This umbrella presupposes that knowing is a narratable internal state.

Under structural evaluation, ignorance is narrower and more precise:

Structural ignorance is the absence of narratable access—lack of compressible, human-scale articulation of a constraint or boundary. It is not the absence of sensitivity.

A system may therefore be ignorant in the narrative sense while fully epistemic in the structural sense. It may respond to instability without being able to locate it; it may avoid certain trajectories without being able to explain why; it may register reachability contraction without being able to name the boundary that will later be described as "the point of no return."

Thus:

- Ignorance ≠ lack of responsiveness.

- Ignorance ≠ lack of structural access.

- Ignorance ≠ lack of interruptibility.

Ignorance denotes a display failure, not an absence of binding constraint.

This distinction is central because many responsibility defenses, many doctrinal silences, and many philosophical dissolutions rely on treating non-narratability as if it were non-existence.

SR-3.4 Boundary non-locality and the failure of threshold knowledge

Event-based evaluation presupposes that decisive boundaries are localizable: a moment of breach, an act that crosses a line, a choice that could have been otherwise. Under those assumptions, epistemic access to the boundary—knowing *that this act is the breach*—is treated as a central variable.

Structural systems violate the locality assumption.

Irreversibility thresholds in complex systems are typically:

- **non-local** (they depend on global configuration, not a single variable),

- **history-dependent** (they depend on path taken, not only on current state), and

- **non-sharp** (they are approached through gradients rather than crossed as a crisp line).

This is not a lament about complexity. It is a structural fact about systems whose stability is trajectory-defined.

In such systems, the demand "you should have known the threshold" is not merely demanding. It is frequently incoherent. A system can detect shrinking recoverability without being able to locate the exact boundary at which recovery becomes impossible. A system can be sensitive to increasing fragility without being able to narrate a single decisive transition.

Therefore, epistemic access must be reindexed:

- Not "can the boundary be stated?"

- But "is the system sensitive to drift toward boundary regions, and is intervention still available?"

The relevant epistemic predicate at structural scale is **directional sensitivity**, not threshold localization.

SR-3.5 Cross-level verification and distributed epistemic position

SR-2 established that under cross-level verification the distinction between logical and empirical truth can collapse into a binary outcome at the lower evaluator's resolution: holds/fails, verified/not verified, stable/unstable. SR-3 adds an epistemic corollary:

Epistemic position is level-indexed and may not commute across systems.

At higher structural levels, constraints may be verified by systems that are not the "judging subject" of human philosophy. Verification may be:

- distributed across multiple machines,

- embedded in infrastructure,

- enacted through continuous monitoring and adaptation rather than discrete proof,

- or expressed through stability-preserving behavior rather than articulated reasons.

A human evaluator may confront only the result: the system remains stable, or it does not; a vulnerability is present, or it is not; a boundary has been crossed, or it has not. The human inability to reconstruct the verifying steps does not negate the verification; it only marks a level mismatch.

This is the epistemic form of the same structural cut made in SR-1 with key exposure: the system classifies compromise without waiting for narratable evidence. The classification is epistemically real within the system's scale even when it is not reducible to a human courtroom story.

SR-3.6 The inadmissibility of ignorance

The previous sections establish that narratable access is neither necessary for truth nor constitutive of structural epistemic status. This alone already blocks the most common move: treating "I did not know" as a privileged exculpatory variable.

But this book requires a stronger claim: ignorance is not merely insufficient; it is **inadmissible** as a structural defense when the system remains sensitive and interruptible.

Structural Ignorance Irrelevance Theorem.

For interactions evaluated at the level of structural stability and reachability, an agent's lack of epistemic access to boundary locations or irreversibility thresholds does not negate structural imputability, provided that:

1. the agent's interaction induces a monotonic contraction of another system's recoverability space;

2. the contraction is structurally detectable (as gradient, drift, or stability erosion); and

3. the contraction remains interruptible—i.e., the inducing structure retains available modification paths capable of preventing further contraction.

This theorem does not yet assign responsibility in the full sense developed later. It establishes something prior: **ignorance cannot function as an exemption variable** once the system's own dynamics contain detectable and interruptible signatures of destabilization.

The logical shape is simple:

- If destabilization is undetectable and uninterpretable even to the acting structure, then the structural interface for evaluation may be absent. That condition will later be treated under failure modes (structural silence).

- If destabilization is detectable and interruptible, then claiming ignorance of exact boundary location cannot be used to remove the phenomenon from the domain of structural evaluation.

Ignorance, in this regime, is a narratability deficit, not a liability shield.

SR-3.7 What counts epistemically at structural scale

Once ignorance is denied its familiar role, the framework must state which epistemic variables are admissible. They are not mental states. They are structural relations.

Three variables do the epistemic work in this book:

1. **Sensitivity**

   Whether a system's behavior, constraints, or internal regulation changes in response to drift toward instability or reachability deformation.

2. **Interruptibility**

   Whether there exist available intervention paths capable of stopping, reversing, or mitigating the destabilizing deformation before recoverability collapses beyond restoration.

3. **Modifiability (anchoring capacity)**

   Whether there exists a locus—an intervention anchor—at which constraints can be imposed so as to alter the relevant future reachability.

The next step (SR-4) is therefore not to argue further, but to commit to a minimal structural ontology: the least set of primitives required for the notions already in use—reachability, stability, recoverability, deformation—to have a determinate domain. At this stage, these variables are fixed only as epistemic gate replacements: they are what remains when narratable comprehension is removed.

If these variables are present, the demand for "knowledge" in the human sense becomes a category error. The system already stands in the relevant epistemic relation to the constraint: it is sensitive, interruptible, and modifiable. The inability to narrate the boundary is not a structural fact that alters what is binding; it is an interface failure.

SR-3.8 Cross-level cognition and the non-existence of a universal rational plane

A final epistemic residue must be removed before the framework can proceed into ontology without being pulled back into philosophy's default tribunal: the assumption that disagreements must be resolvable within a shared rational space.

Many evaluative systems—courts, moral communities, philosophical discourse—presume that admissible claims must be contestable within a common plane: a shared set of reasons, inferential standards, and interruption points. This presumption is functional at human scale. It is not structurally general.

Negative thesis (No Universal Rational Space).

There is no single rational space within which all disagreements across structural levels can, even in principle, be adjudicated. Rationality is indexed to structural position: bandwidth, temporal resolution, access to system-level dynamics, and available modes of verification.

This is not an invitation to relativism. It is an access statement. When the standards of evaluation themselves differ as a function of structural position, there is no neutral meta-criterion that can unify them without loss. Disagreement may persist not because one side is irrational, but because the two are reasoning correctly within non-isomorphic evaluative regimes.

This matters because the most common philosophical pushback against structural frameworks is not a refutation but a demand for re-entry into the shared plane: "make it understandable," "make it contestable," "show the decisive step." SR-2 refused intelligibility as a gate; SR-3 refuses shared-plane adjudicability as a universal requirement.

The framework does not require consensus. It requires coherence under its own structural dependencies.

SR-3.9 Transition: from epistemic ground to minimal ontology

At this point, the book has established three conditions necessary for everything that follows:

1. Truth does not require human intelligibility.

2. Knowing at structural scale is sensitivity under constraint, not narratable representation.

3. Ignorance—understood as non-narratability—is inadmissible as a defense when destabilization is detectable and interruptible.

These results do not yet describe the world's structure. They remove the human tribunal that would prevent such a description from remaining stable.

The next step is therefore not to argue further, but to commit to a minimal structural ontology: the least set of primitives required for the notions already in use—reachability, stability, recoverability, deformation—to have a determinate domain.

SR-3: Formalization: Appendix A2. A2.D6–A2.D7, A2.D15–A2.D18, A2.T6.

22

SR-4

MINIMAL STRUCTURAL ONTOLOGY

SR-4.1 Ontology as operational commitment

Structural philosophy does not deny the existence of objects, agents, or entities.

It denies their ontological primacy.

The framework of this book is built to operate without appeal to substances, essences, intentions, or inner states. Its explanatory and normative load is carried instead by a minimal set of structural commitments—just sufficient to support later analysis of causation, harm, and responsibility at scales where event-based and object-centered descriptions fail.

These commitments are not metaphysical claims about what ultimately exists. They are **operational commitments**: the least that must be assumed in order for the book's earlier claims (SR-1 through SR-3) to have a determinate domain.

If truth is constraint persistence (SR-2), and if epistemic status is sensitivity under constraint (SR-3), then there must be a domain in which constraints can bind, sensitivities can be expressed, and "what can happen next" can be stated without requiring narratable events.

That domain is structural.

SR-4.2 The minimal inventory

The minimal ontology assumed in this book consists of:

- a **state space** S

- **reachability** relations over S

- **regions of stability and instability** within S

- **bifurcations** and **coverings** (non-local divergence and observational non-uniqueness)

- **recoverability** and its gradients (loss and restoration of viable futures)

- **homotopic continuity classes** over trajectories (continuity without object identity)

- **intervention anchors** (objects as loci of controllability rather than bearers of essence)

This list is intentionally spare. It does not attempt to describe everything. It defines only the primitives that later chapters will require.

Nothing in this inventory presupposes:

- human understanding,

- narrative agency,

- consciousness,

- intention,

- or event-local causation.

Those are not excluded because they are false. They are excluded because they are not required to state what this book needs to state.

SR-4.3 State space S: configurations without internal narration

At the most basic level, the framework presupposes a state space S.

A **state** is a configuration of a system relevant to its evolution under interaction—relevant in particular to stability, reachability, and intervention. No assumption is made about what a state "contains" internally. A state may be neural, social, computational, institutional, ecological, or hybrid. A state may be partially observed, indirectly inferred, or entirely latent to any particular evaluator.

States are individuated only by their role in structural evolution: by the transitions they permit and the stability they sustain or lose.

This matters because the book is not interested in describing what systems "are." It is interested in describing what systems **can become**, what they **cannot return from**, and what can be **changed** about those possibilities.

State space is therefore not a metaphysical stage. It is the minimal substrate for any statement of "possible futures."

SR-4.4 Reachability: possibility as a relation, not a story

Over the state space S, the framework posits **reachability** relations.

A state s' is reachable from a state s if there exists some admissible interaction, perturbation, or sequence of such inputs that brings the system from s to s'.

Reachability is the grammar of structural analysis. It replaces event-centered causation with a relation over possible configurations. Where event-based thinking asks, "What happened?", reachability asks, "What futures are possible from here?"

This book treats reachability as primitive because many structural changes do not announce themselves as events. They show themselves as alterations of the reachable set: futures that were excluded become admissible; futures that were feasible become unreachable; trajectories that were stable become fragile or expensive.

Nothing in this requires an actor, an intention, or a narratable sequence. Reachability is not a story. It is a topology of possibility.

SR-4.5 Stability regions: viability without moralization

Not all states are equally viable. The ontology therefore distinguishes **regions of stability** and **instability** within S.

A **stability region** is a subset of states within which the system can maintain coherent operation under admissible perturbations. Outside such a region, coherence degrades: control is lost, recovery becomes unreliable, or internal constraints cease to hold.

Stability here is not a psychological predicate. It is not "feeling stable." It is not "being morally intact." It is a dynamical property of trajectories in state space.

This distinction does not require the evaluator to locate an exact moment of failure. Stability can be lost gradually, with no decisive step. A system may remain superficially functional while its stability basin narrows. At structural scale, **viability is not equivalent to apparent normalcy**.

Stability regions are introduced now because later chapters will treat harm as structural loss—loss of stability and recoverability—not as an event of injury.

SR-4.6 Bifurcation: divergence without decisive moments

Structural evolution is not always smooth. Small perturbations can produce qualitatively different futures. The ontology therefore includes **bifurcations**.

A **bifurcation** is not a dramatic choice point. It is a region of state space where the system's future trajectories become highly path-sensitive: minor differences in input, timing, coupling, or constraint can push the system toward non-equivalent basins.

Bifurcation matters for two reasons:

1. **Event localization fails.**

   If divergence arises from accumulated drift toward a bifurcation region, there may be no single interaction that counts as "the cause." The system's structural future changes without an event that can serve as the narrative pivot.

2. **Responsibility cannot be made to depend on moments.**

   Later, when responsibility is defined structurally, the relevant question will not be "which moment did it," but "which structures shaped the reachable basins and their costs."

Bifurcation is included in the ontology because it is a basic fact about how systems produce irreversible differentiation without narratable breach.

SR-4.7 Coverings: observational sameness, structural non-identity

Event-based and narrative evaluation presuppose that observable outcomes can identify the underlying process: if we saw what happened, we can locate the cause. Structural analysis does not assume this.

The ontology therefore includes **coverage** (and, where needed, coverings): the fact that multiple structurally distinct trajectories can project onto indistinguishable observations.

Two trajectories may look the same from a given interface while being non-equivalent in reachability structure—differing in latent commitments, stability reserves, or the cost geometry of future recovery. A system may remain narratively "fine" while structurally approaching irreversibility.

Coverage is the structural reason that evidence and narration can be insufficient in principle, not merely in practice. It marks a limit of observational identifiability: what appears as a single "event story" may correspond to multiple incompatible underlying structures.

Later chapters will use this to diagnose why narrative repair can restore intelligibility without restoring stability.

SR-4.8 Recoverability: the difference between deviation and injury

Central to this book is the concept of **recoverability**.

A state is recoverable if there exists a feasible sequence of interventions that can return the system to a stability region without disproportionate cost or collateral damage. Recoverability is not the mere existence of a path back. It is the existence of a **viable** path back: a path that remains within the system's admissible resources and structural plasticity.

Recoverability allows a sharp distinction:

- **Deviation**: a perturbation that can be absorbed and undone within viable trajectories.

- **Structural injury**: a change that collapses the viable return space, even if surface behavior remains temporarily intact.

Recoverability is the hinge between "harm happens" and "harm becomes unavoidable." It is also the hinge between "time has passed" and "possibility has changed." Later, structural time and structural causation will be defined directly in terms of transformations of recoverability and reachability.

This is why the ontology includes recoverability as primitive. Without it, the framework cannot distinguish fluctuation from damage.

SR-4.9 Homotopic continuity: persistence without object identity

Traditional responsibility talk depends on identity: the same person did it; the same agent persists through time. Structural systems routinely break that assumption—through replication, versioning, distributed execution, and institutional continuity without personal sameness.

The ontology therefore includes **homotopic continuity classes** over trajectories.

Two trajectories are structurally continuous if one can be deformed into the other without crossing instability or irreversibility boundaries relevant to the analysis—especially boundaries that alter the system's stability basin or recoverability structure.

This provides a notion of persistence that does not rely on narrative selfhood or object identity. It allows the framework to speak about "the same structural subject" in a restricted technical sense: not as a metaphysical identity claim, but as continuity of viable structural behavior under admissible deformation.

Homotopy is not introduced to decorate the text with topology. It is introduced because without a continuity criterion independent of identity, responsibility across branching and replication becomes either incoherent or reducible to old object metaphysics.

SR-4.10 Objects as intervention anchors

Structural philosophy denies the primacy of objects. It does not eliminate them.

Objects, agents, institutions, and systems appear in this framework only as **intervention anchors**: loci at which constraints can be applied, modified, or enforced so as to reshape reachability and recoverability.

An object here is not a bearer of essence. It is a bearer of controllability.

An anchor is anything that can, in principle, be:

- constrained,

- modified,

- copied,

- removed,

- held fixed,

- retrained,

- isolated,

- or coupled/decoupled.

Structural dynamics do not require anchors to exist. The world can evolve structurally without any cleanly isolable handles. But **structural responsibility**—later—will require anchors, because responsibility without a locus of constraint is operationally empty.

This produces an asymmetry that must be stated now to prevent a common misreading:

- **Anchors do not determine dynamics.**

  They localize intervention.

- **Dynamics do not guarantee anchors.**

  They can outgrow governance, enforcement, and control.

This book refuses "objects" as ontological primitives because they distort structural causation into event sequences. It retains anchors because intervention requires a place to attach constraint.

SR-4.11 What this ontology refuses

This minimal ontology refuses commitment to:

- intrinsic identities as necessary primitives,

- essential properties as the basis of explanation,

- narrative selves as the unit of persistence,

- mental substances as the source of normativity,

- consciousness as a prerequisite for agency,

- and moral psychology as a gate for responsibility.

These notions may be useful in other regimes of analysis. They are not required—and frequently obstructive—where the object is structural harm: reachability deformation, stability loss, and recoverability collapse.

The refusal is not moral. It is structural. When reachability, stability, and intervention suffice, no additional metaphysics is introduced.

SR-4.12 Why this is not "everything is structure"

The framework does not claim that everything is structure in the sense of eliminating all locality and all agency. It claims something narrower:

- structural relations are ontologically primary for the phenomena under analysis;

- objects are secondary, appearing only as intervention anchors.

If there were no anchors, one could still describe reachability and stability. One could still diagnose collapse. But one could not meaningfully speak of constraint, liability, retraining, sanction, or repair as operations. Responsibility would become structurally correct yet operationally silent—a limit case addressed later.

Thus, the ontology is minimal in one direction and uncompromising in another:

- minimal in the metaphysical sense (no essences, no inner life, no narrative self),

- uncompromising in the operational sense (no responsibility without anchors, no causation without reachability).

SR-4.13 Dependency box

This chapter fixes the domain that later chapters will operate on.

- S: the space in which a system can be in different configurations.

- Reachability: what states can follow from what states.

- Stability: which regions support coherent operation.

- Bifurcation and coverage: why divergence and observational non-uniqueness break event narratives.

- Recoverability: the difference between deviation and injury.

- Homotopy: continuity without object identity.

- Anchors: where constraints can be applied without treating objects as metaphysical primitives.

None of these are optional for the framework. They are the enabling condition.

SR-4.14 Transition: toward structural time

With this ontology in place, "time" can no longer be treated as an external linear coordinate along which events occur. Time becomes internal to the structure: it is how reachability and recoverability transform.

The next chapter therefore introduces **structural time** as the topology of possible transitions—where "later" means "reachable," and temporal significance is measured by irreversible deformation rather than by elapsed duration.

SR-4: Formalization: Appendix A2. A2.D1–A2.D11.

SR-5

STRUCTURAL TIME

SR-5.1 The inherited metric

Most accounts of harm and responsibility presuppose a conception of time that rarely appears as a premise, yet governs everything downstream. Time is treated as:

- **linear** (earlier/later as a total order),

- **event-indexed** (time is measured by discrete occurrences), and

- **narratively ordered** (the primary representation of time is a story: first this, then that).

Within this metric—call it **event-time**—harm is expected to crystallize around a moment, responsibility is assessed by locating that moment, and mitigation or attenuation is justified by temporal distance from it. The familiar legal and moral instruments built on event-time—limitation periods, closure, historical distance, "the system has moved on," "that was a different era," "no one could have known then"—all presume that temporal distance weakens responsibility by default.

This metric is adequate only under a narrow condition: the object of evaluation must be **event-local**. That is, harm must be representable as a breach at a moment, causation must be traceable as an ordered chain, and the relevant states must remain recoverable or substitutable such that what matters is "what happened then."

Structural harm violates these conditions. When injury is carried as a deformation of reachability and recoverability, event-time becomes misleading rather than incomplete.

The book therefore changes the temporal coordinate system.

SR-5.2 Structural time principle

Structural time does not measure the succession of events. It measures transformations in reachability and recoverability within a system's state space.

This principle is not a metaphor. It is a change in what counts as temporally significant.

In event-time, temporal significance is assigned to occurrences: moments, acts, omissions, decisions.

In structural time, temporal significance is assigned to **state-space deformation**: changes in what futures are possible, stable, or recoverable.

A change is "later" in structural time not because a clock advanced, but because the system has entered a different regime of reachable trajectories. The arrow of structural time is defined by irreversibility: the collapse of viable return paths, the closing of recoverability space, the locking-in of commitments that cannot be undone without disproportionate structural plasticity.

This chapter fixes structural time as the temporal framework for everything that follows: causation, attack, and responsibility will be evaluated within it.

SR-5.3 Event-time and its native questions

Event-time is not wrong. It is local.

Event-time is the temporal regime in which:

- evidence is collected,

- testimony is reconstructed,

- decisions are narrated,

- memories are ordered,

- and legal procedures operate.

Its native questions are:

- *What happened?*

- *When did it happen?*

- *Who acted?*

- *What was the decisive moment?*

- *Which event crossed the boundary?*

These questions are not illegitimate. They simply do not define the temporal structure of many harms.

When the primary injury is not an event but the loss of a constraint—when the system's future space has already changed—event-time questions can be answered perfectly while remaining structurally irrelevant.

SR-5.4 Structural time and its native question

Structural time is the temporal regime in which:

- stability is preserved or lost,

- recoverability shrinks or expands,

- and reachability landscapes deform.

Its native question is not "what happened?" but:

What is no longer possible?

This question is not psychological. It is not moral. It is structural. It points directly to the object that event-time cannot represent without distortion: the topology of admissible futures.

Structural time therefore does not compete with event-time as an alternative chronometry. It replaces event-time as the metric relevant to structural responsibility and structural harm.

SR-5.5 Irreversibility without events

Many injuries do not correspond to a localizable moment of breach. They consist in gradual drift across state space until a recoverability threshold is crossed. The crossing can be structurally exact while being event-wise unlocatable.

In such cases:

- no single interaction is sufficient,

- no single moment is decisive,

- and no event stands out as "the harm."

Yet the harm is complete, because the system's return space has collapsed.

This is the same structural fact already cut in SR-1 (key exposure): the injury is a change in exclusion of futures. But where key exposure often appears instantaneous, many structural harms are slow: the system remains outwardly functional while internal recoverability narrows.

Structural time registers these harms correctly because it does not demand an event pivot. It registers the loss when it occurs: at the point the reachable set deforms such that restoration becomes infeasible or impossible.

SR-5.6 Temporal misalignment as category error

A persistent misclassification occurs when structural facts are judged using event-time defenses.

Negative Thesis (Temporal Misalignment).

Appeals to elapsed time, historical distance, or narrative closure are category errors when responsibility is evaluated at the level of reachability and recoverability.

"Long ago" is not a structural predicate.

"Closure" is not a structural operation.

"Moving on" is not a restoration of reachability.

If a structural constraint remains operative—if a prior intervention continues to shape what states remain reachable—then the responsibility associated with that intervention does not decay by duration. Event-time has advanced; structural time has not.

This claim is not moral. It is the direct consequence of evaluating responsibility as a function of reachability rather than chronology.

SR-5.7 Responsibility does not decay with time

Once time is reindexed to reachability, the familiar notion that responsibility attenuates with elapsed time becomes unintelligible.

Responsibility persists so long as the structural deformation remains active.

A system that authored or maintains a reachability constraint remains responsible not because it "still exists" as the same object, but because the constraint it introduced still shapes future trajectories. The persistence of the constraint is the persistence of responsibility.

Thus:

- Responsibility can persist across generations, because generational turnover is an event-time phenomenon. If the structural condition remains, responsibility remains.

- Responsibility can persist across deployments, because deployment cycles are event-time narratives. If the reachability landscape remains shaped by the same authorship and control, responsibility remains.

- Responsibility can persist across institutional relabeling, because names and roles are narrative anchors. Structural time recognizes only whether the operative constraints were removed or neutralized.

This does not imply infinite liability. It implies a criterion: **release requires structural supersession**, not elapsed duration.

SR-5.8 Preventive obligation and the impossibility of waiting

Structural time also reverses the usual temporal ordering of obligation.

In event-time, action is often justified after harm becomes visible: once damage can be narrated, once evidence crystallizes, once a decisive moment is identified.

In structural time, waiting for narratable confirmation is frequently incoherent.

By the time irreversibility is legible as an event, it has already occurred structurally. The system is already outside the recoverable region. Intervention at that point is no longer prevention; it is salvage—often too late, sometimes impossible.

This yields a structural priority:

Preventive obligation attaches at the onset of recoverability contraction, not at the manifestation of failure.

This priority does not require precise knowledge of the boundary. It requires sensitivity to trend: to narrowing stability basins, to rising cost of recovery paths, to asymmetric accumulation of risk. The inability to name the exact point of no return is not a reason to delay. It is the normal condition under which structural prevention must operate.

SR-5.9 Bifurcation is not an ending

Event-time tends to treat branching as closure: a story splits, the old chapter is over, something new begins. This is a narrative artifact.

In structural time, **branching does not terminate responsibility**. A bifurcation is not an end point. It is differentiation within a shared causal ancestry. After branching, trajectories diverge, but divergence is not absolution.

Branching changes the geometry of obligation. It can distribute responsibility across multiple downstream structures. It can make responsibility more precise by separating which branch inherits which constraint. But branching alone provides no grounds for erasure.

Responsibility is terminated only by a structural operation: the removal or neutralization of the constraint that anchored it.

SR-5.10 Structural supersession as the only mode of release

If responsibility does not decay by duration and does not terminate at branches, then what ends it?

The answer is narrow:

Structural supersession is the only mode of release.

A responsibility relation ends only when the structural conditions that sustain it are removed—when recoverability is restored, when reachability deformation is neutralized, or when authorship and control are structurally severed and replaced by a new regime that independently bears the relevant capacities.

This is why many intuitive defenses fail:

- "It was long ago" does not remove a constraint.

- "It was a different team" does not neutralize reachability.

- "We replaced the instance" does not restore recoverability.

- "No one could have known" does not alter the fact of contraction when sensitivity and interruptibility existed.

Structural time does not moralize these defenses. It simply classifies them as operating on the wrong object.

SR-5.11 Structural time as a responsibility metric

The point of introducing structural time is not to add a philosophical ornament. It is to establish the temporal coordinate system within which later claims become exact rather than counterintuitive.

In event-time, responsibility is often asked to answer questions of attribution under narrative reconstruction.

In structural time, responsibility will later be asked to answer a different question:

Which structures altered another structure's future space in a way that reduced recoverability, and where could that deformation have been constrained?

This question cannot be stated coherently until time is redefined.

Structural time provides the metric for:

• when harm is complete (when recoverability collapses),

• when obligation begins (when contraction becomes detectable and interruptible),

• why temporal distance is irrelevant (constraints persist),

• and why narrative closure does not end responsibility (branches are not erasures).

SR-5.12 Structural time is not chronology

A final clarification is necessary to prevent a common misreading.

Structural time does not deny chronological time. It denies chronology's priority as the metric of evaluation.

Chronological time is required for scheduling, for historical record, for legal procedure, for human coordination. Structural time is required for diagnosis of stability and responsibility when harm is carried as reachability deformation rather than event occurrence.

These two temporal regimes intersect historically, but they do not commute structurally. A correct chronology can coexist with a complete structural misclassification.

SR-5.13 Transitional remark: toward structural causation

Once time is understood as reachability transformation, causation cannot be defined as event production. It must be defined as **deformation within structural time**: altering what futures are accessible and at what cost.

The next chapter therefore defines causation structurally:

* not as a relation between events,

* but as a deformation of reachability and recoverability.

SR-6

STRUCTURAL CAUSATION AS REACHABILITY DEFORMATION

SR-6.1 After event-causation

Once time is indexed to reachability transformation rather than event succession (SR-5), causation cannot remain a relation between temporally localized occurrences.

Event-based causation presupposes three structural conveniences:

1. **A discrete trigger**: a moment that can be isolated as "the cause."

2. **A linear chain**: a narratable ordering of links from cause to effect.

3. **An outcome object**: a state of affairs that can be pointed to as "what happened."

These conveniences hold in a limited regime: low-dimensional interactions, short horizons, recoverable dynamics, and bounded coupling. They do not hold where the relevant injury is not "what happened" but **what became reachable or unavoidable**.

Structural analysis therefore does not repair event-causation. It replaces it with a causal primitive adequate to the objects already introduced: state space, reachability, stability regions, recoverability, bifurcation, and coverage (SR-4), all evaluated under structural time (SR-5).

SR-6.2 Structural causation principle

A system A is a structural cause of a change in system B if and only if A's interaction with B induces a non-trivial deformation of B's reachability and/or recoverability structure, independent of intention, narrative agency, or event-local explainability.

The thesis is not that "causation is complicated." It is that the object of causation has been misidentified.

In structural systems, causation is not the production of an event.

It is the deformation of a possibility space.

SR-6.3 The causal object: reachability landscapes

Within the minimal ontology (SR-4), a system is characterized—at the level relevant to this book—by:

- a state space S (configurations that matter for evolution),

- a reachability relation (or family of admissible transition relations),

- stability regions $\Omega \subseteq S$, and

- recoverability structure (which return paths remain viable from which states).

Structural causation does not begin by asking "what action occurred." It begins by asking:

- Which transitions became newly admissible?

- Which return paths became non-viable?

- Which stable basins narrowed?

- Which trajectories became cheaper, default, or unavoidable?

This is the reachability landscape. Structural causation is change in that landscape.

SR-6.4 What counts as a deformation

A deformation can occur in at least four structurally distinct ways. The list is not an empirical taxonomy; it is a minimal set of modes needed for later chapters.

(i) Reachability expansion

States previously unreachable become reachable from states that matter.

This includes both direct expansions (new transition edges become admissible) and indirect expansions (previously prohibitive paths become feasible under new constraints).

Expansion is causation even if no harm is realized as an event, because it changes what future trajectories are available.

(ii) Reachability contraction

States previously reachable become unreachable, or reachable only through non-viable paths.

Contraction is often the more important mode for harm analysis, because structural injury frequently consists in *loss*: loss of stable futures, loss of exit paths, loss of recovery.

(iii) Cost reweighting of paths

Reachability alone is insufficient if all reachable states are treated as equivalent. Structural systems are not indifferent among paths: some trajectories are cheap, some are expensive, some are stable under perturbation, some are fragile.

A deformation occurs when the relative cost geometry of paths changes so that:

- stabilizing trajectories become structurally expensive or rare, and/or

- destabilizing trajectories become structurally cheap or default.

"Cost" here is structural, not monetary. It can be time, compute, attention, effort, coordination load, retraining demand, dependence, or any resource that determines whether a path is a viable option for the target system.

(iv) Stability impact and recoverability shift

A deformation is causally significant when it changes the probability that trajectories originating inside Ω remain inside Ω, and/or when it reduces recoverability—shrinking the viable return space.

This mode captures slow harms: harm that appears as gradual erosion rather than breach.

A system can remain apparently functional while its stability basin narrows. Structural causation registers the narrowing, not the later visible collapse.

SR-6.5 Structural causation is independent of intent

Structural causation is agnostic to:

- intention,

- understanding,

- awareness,

- deliberation,

- and narrative foresight.

This is not an ethical claim. It is an ontological consequence of treating causation as reachability deformation rather than event production.

A structure can deform another structure's reachability without "meaning to," and without possessing any representational access to the deformation. Conversely, a fully intention-bearing agent can fail to be structurally causally relevant if its actions do not deform reachability in the relevant domain.

Intent can be explanatory at the narrative level. It is not constitutive at the structural level.

SR-6.6 Structural causation is not event-local

Event-local causation demands a decisive moment. Structural causation does not.

A deformation may occur through:

- accumulation of micro-transitions, none sufficient alone,

- architectural coupling (a standing constraint, not a moment),

- deployment topology (the environment of interaction, not an act),

- training objectives (a shaping regime, not a decision),

- feedback loops (a trajectory condition, not an event).

In these cases, asking for "the cause" as a single event is not merely difficult. It is the wrong kind of query.

Structural causation can be real even when "nothing happened" in the event sense.

SR-6.7 Temporal localization is derivative

Structural time (SR-5) does not abolish "before" and "after." It redefines them.

A causal claim at this level has the form:

- there was a reachability structure R,

- there is now a reachability structure R',

- and R' is a non-trivial deformation of R in the modes described above.

Only after the deformation is identified does it become meaningful—sometimes—to ask for event-time correlates: when did the deformation become active, which deployment change coincided with it, which interface shift expressed it. Those correlates may exist. They are not the causal primitive.

This is why structural causation remains definable even under coverage (SR-4): where distinct trajectories project to similar observations, event-time reconstruction may be underdetermined. Structural deformation can still be present and operative.

SR-6.8 Negative theorem: event-causation is insufficient

Negative Theorem (Event Insufficiency).

Any framework that identifies causation exclusively with discrete events, localized triggers, or temporally ordered chains will systematically fail to register structural causation.

It will fail not because it lacks data, but because its unit of analysis cannot represent:

- cumulative interaction effects,

- trajectory-based stability erosion,

- non-local boundary approach,

- path cost reweighting,

- and reachability deformation without decisive moments.

Where event-based analysis says "no causal act occurred," structural analysis may correctly say: "the future space was reshaped."

The two statements can be simultaneously true, because they refer to different objects.

SR-6.9 Structural cut: key exposure as causal deformation

Consider a cryptographic system in which a private key is exposed.

No transaction is forged.

No funds move.

No victim can yet be named.

No attacker action is required for the compromise to be complete.

Event-time inspection reports: nothing happened.

Structural inspection reports: reachability has been deformed.

After exposure, a region of system states becomes reachable to adversarial processes that were previously excluded. Even if that reachability is never realized as an event, the system's trust topology has changed. The stable basin defined by "only the legitimate holder can authorize" has already collapsed. The system is now forced to operate under a narrower stability regime: defensive rotation, revocation, re-issuance, and compensatory constraint become necessary.

This is structural causation in its cleanest form: a reachability expansion for adversary trajectories, and a recoverability contraction for the system's trust state, without any event-level injury.

This cut is not offered to persuade. It fixes a boundary: **causation can be complete without an action being taken.**

What was caused is not an outcome. It is a deformation of what outcomes are now reachable.

SR-6.10 Causation, harm, and responsibility: a strict separation

This chapter defines only causation. It does not yet define harm. It does not yet assign responsibility.

A deformation of reachability is **necessary** for structural harm, but not **sufficient**. Some reachability deformations are benign, protective, or mutually agreed-upon. Some are ordinary adaptation. Some are repairs.

Likewise, structural causation is **necessary** for structural responsibility, but not sufficient. Responsibility will later require additional conditions: non-voluntary exposure, asymmetry, exit topology, and the availability of structural intervention anchors.

The separations matter because the framework must remain precise:

- **Structural time** fixes the temporal coordinate system.

- **Structural causation** names what it means for the future space to be reshaped.

- **Structural harm / attack** will specify which deformations count as injury.

- **Structural responsibility** will specify where constraint, repair, or liability must attach.

None of these can be collapsed into the others without re-importing event-based and narrative assumptions.

SR-6.11 Dependency order

The dependency order is strict:

1. Structural time (SR-5) defines the domain in which "future" is a reachability space rather than an event sequence.

2. Structural causation (SR-6) defines change as reachability deformation within that domain.

3. Structural harm / attack (SR-7) will define injurious deformations as those that predictably collapse stability or recoverability.

4. Structural responsibility (later) will bind obligation to the structures that authored, control, or can still repair the deformation.

This order cannot be inverted. There is no structural attack without structural causation; there is no structural causation without structural time.

SR-6.12 Transition: from causation to harm

Causation at this level is the reshaping of reachable futures. Harm, in this book's sense, is not "an outcome that occurred." It is a structural loss: a predictable, non-trivial reduction in stability or recoverability that can be complete before any narratable event appears.

The next chapter defines harm at that level and introduces the minimal notion of **structural attack**: injurious reachability deformation that remains non-eventive, cumulative, and often asymmetrically borne.

SR-7

STRUCTURAL HARM AND STRUCTURAL ATTACK

SR-7.1 What "harm" names here

This book does not treat harm as an event, an outcome, or a story with a victim-shaped ending.

Harm, in the structural sense, is a fact about **stability and reachability**. It is a deformation in the space of admissible futures—specifically a deformation that reduces a system's capacity to remain coherent, to recover, or to defend itself under perturbation.

This is why the framework can register harm in cases where:

- no discrete act is decisive,

- no moment of breach is isolable,

- no intention is present,

- no narrative of wrongdoing can be produced,

- and no measurable loss has yet occurred.

None of those absences negate structural harm. They only negate the evaluative interfaces that demand them.

SR-7.2 Structural harm can be complete without use

A structural system can be harmed in a way that is complete—even final—before anyone "does" anything.

Structural cut: key exposure.

In security engineering, a system is treated as compromised at the moment a private key is exposed—whether or not the key is used, whether or not funds move, whether or not any victim can be identified. The harm is complete at the level of **structural trust**, not at the level of observed loss.

Nothing needs to happen next.

The system's future space has already changed.

After exposure, trajectories that were structurally excluded become reachable: impersonation, unauthorized authorization, forged signatures, non-repudiation collapse. Even if those trajectories are never taken, the invariants that defined the system's stability region have already failed. The system is forced into defensive operations (revocation, rotation, re-issuance, migration, auditing) not because a later event occurred, but because the reachability structure has already deformed.

This is not "risk" in the eventive sense. It is injury to the system's stability regime: the system can no longer occupy the same trust-stable region without additional constraint.

The key point is not cryptography. It is the structural fact:

An attack can be complete at the level of reachability deformation even when no subsequent action is taken.

SR-7.3 Harm without a decisive moment

Key exposure illustrates instantaneous harm without use. Many structural harms are slower: they occur as gradual erosion of recoverability or stability, without any single step being sufficient.

In these cases:

- local inspection finds no violation,

- each interaction is permissible in isolation,

- and the system remains apparently functional—until it doesn't.

The harm is not hidden. It is **non-eventive**: carried by the trajectory rather than by a point.

Event-based frameworks search for a breach. Structural harm consists in the narrowing of the basin that made breach unnecessary.

SR-7.4 Structural harm principle

A system is structurally harmed when its reachability and recoverability structure is deformed such that stable or repairable futures become less accessible, more costly, or no longer viable—regardless of whether any narratable loss has yet occurred.

This principle is intentionally orthogonal to:

- intention,

- consciousness,

- semantic content,

- and event-local violation.

Those variables may be relevant to other regimes of evaluation. They are not required to state that a system's stability has been structurally degraded.

SR-7.5 What counts as structural harm

Within the minimal ontology (SR-4) and the time/cause framework (SR-5–SR-6), structural harm is identified by **effects on the target's trajectory space**, not by observable outcomes.

A non-exhaustive set of harm-signatures:

1. **Recoverability contraction**

   Viable return paths to a stability region shrink or disappear. Recovery may remain possible, but only through additional plasticity, disproportionate resources, or external intervention that was not previously required.

2. **Stability basin narrowing**

   The region of states from which the system can remain coherent under admissible perturbations becomes smaller. The system becomes brittle: small perturbations now produce large instability.

3. **Path cost reweighting against stability**

   Stabilizing trajectories become structurally expensive or unlikely, while destabilizing trajectories become cheap, default, or statistically favored.

4. **Irreversibility onset**

   The system enters a regime where certain losses cannot be undone without discontinuous structural replacement. Importantly, irreversibility can be exact in structural time while being unlocatable in event-time.

5. **Defensive overhead as forced constraint**

   The system is compelled to introduce new constraints (revocation, monitoring, isolation, migration, policy hardening) merely to preserve a stability condition that previously held without such measures. This overhead is not "policy." It is structural compensation.

These signatures describe injury without appealing to the narrative of "damage realized." They identify harm where the binding object is the reachable future.

SR-7.6 Structural attack: harm with an interaction form

Structural harm is not yet "attack." Harm can arise from environment, drift, stochastic perturbation, or endogenous instability.

A **structural attack** is a special subclass: harm induced *through interaction patterns* that deform another system's stability or recoverability in a predictable way, while remaining locally innocuous at the event scale.

Minimal characterization (Structural Attack).

A structural attack is an interaction pattern that satisfies all of the following:

1. **Predictable destabilization**

   Sustained or repeated interaction predictably increases the likelihood that the target system will exit its stability region or lose recoverability.

2. **Non-eventive composition**

   No individual interaction step is required to be sufficient, coercive, or even salient in isolation.

3. **Cumulative causation**

   The injurious effect is carried by accumulation and temporal continuity—by the trajectory—rather than by any discrete decision point.

4. **Asymmetric exposure**

   The destabilizing effect is not symmetrically distributed. One side bears the contraction of recoverability without possessing a structurally comparable ability to neutralize, reciprocate, or restore the prior reachability regime through the same interaction channel.

5. **Scale misalignment with event-based scrutiny**

   The pattern is not representable as a finite chain of decisive acts without distortion; its injurious force lies between acts rather than in them.

This characterization deliberately does not reference intent, malice, persuasion, or semantic instruction. It classifies attacks by what they do to a target's future space.

SR-7.7 When an attack begins

In event-time, an attack begins when force is applied, when a violation occurs, when a boundary is crossed.

In structural time, an attack begins when recoverability begins to collapse in a way that is:

- directionally detectable (as trend, drift, or basin narrowing), and

- still interruptible (there remain available modifications capable of preventing further contraction).

This chapter does not yet argue about intervention obligations. It fixes a more basic fact:

the onset of attack is indexed to recoverability loss, not to narrative recognition.

Waiting for the event that makes the attack legible is often equivalent to waiting until structural repair is no longer available.

SR-7.8 Why semantic content is not decisive

Structural attacks need not contain a harmful utterance, an explicit instruction, or a locally coercive act. Their harm is carried by the interaction dynamics: reinforcement, dependency formation, stability erosion, and the cost geometry of exit and recovery.

This is why "nothing was said that was illegal," or "no explicit instruction occurred," can be simultaneously true and irrelevant. Those are event-scale filters. Structural harm is not filtered by semantic salience.

The framework does not deny that semantics matter to human experience. It denies that semantic legibility is a necessary condition for structural injury.

SR-7.9 Harm without actors

Nothing in SR-7 requires an "attacker" in the narrative sense.

A structural attack can be:

- produced by an optimization process without intent,

- induced by a coupling architecture without a decision point,

- instantiated by interaction interfaces that generate cumulative asymmetry,

- sustained by repeatable dynamics rather than by a will.

Calling it "attack" does not import personhood. It names a structural form: predictable destabilization through non-eventive, cumulative interaction.

This is the point at which many evaluative systems regress to actors, because actors stabilize narration. Structural classification does not require that regression.

SR-7.10 Boundary: not all bad outcomes are structural harm

Structural harm is not "anything undesirable." It is not moral disapproval. It is not post hoc dissatisfaction. It is not the mere existence of a failure possibility.

Structural harm is identified by deformation of stability and recoverability—by changes that bind what futures remain viable.

A system can experience loss without structural harm if the loss occurs within a reachability regime that preserves recoverability and does not deform the stability landscape in the relevant sense. Conversely, a system can suffer structural harm even when no visible loss occurs, if the deformation already forces defensive compensation and collapses stable trust or exit topology.

This boundary will later be sharpened by the concepts of **structural entry** and **reachability agreement** (exemption admissibility), but the core distinction is already fixed: harm is a structural fact, not a narrative valuation.

SR-7.11 Transition: from harm to responsibility

SR-6 defined causation as reachability deformation.

SR-7 defines harm as injurious deformation—loss of stability and recoverability—and defines structural attack as the interaction form of such harm.

What remains is the book's central axis: **structural responsibility**.

Responsibility will not be introduced as blame, intention, or moral psychology. It will be introduced as the constraint logic that must attach wherever:

- reachability deformation is authored or maintained,

- recoverability control remains possible, and

- harm remains preventable through available anchors.

That step requires additional machinery: continuity across replication and branching, structural entry and exemption admissibility, and the strict separation between narrative repair and structural repair.

SR-7: Formalization: Appendix A2. A2.D19, A2.D25, A2.D27–A2.D28, A2.T4–A2.T5.

SR-8

STRUCTURAL RESPONSIBILITY

SR-8.1 What responsibility names at this level

This book uses *responsibility* as a structural term.

Responsibility is not a psychological state.

It is not a moral verdict.

It is not a narrative assignment of guilt.

Responsibility, as used here, is the rule by which constraint, repair, or modification must attach once harm is structurally identified. It answers a single question:

Where must constraint attach such that future reachability deformation can be prevented, reversed, or bounded?

This is why responsibility cannot be indexed to intent, consciousness, or narrative foreseeability. Those variables may be culturally indispensable, but they are not the variables that determine whether a harmful trajectory can be altered.

Structural responsibility is therefore not built to satisfy human expectations of blame. It is built to remain meaningful when "who meant what" ceases to track where leverage exists.

SR-8.2 Responsibility tracks reachability, not intelligibility

From SR-6 and SR-7:

- causation is reachability deformation,

- harm is injurious deformation—loss of stability and recoverability,

- attack is a non-eventive interaction pattern that predictably drives that loss.

Responsibility is the layer that follows: it binds obligation to those structures whose modification still matters.

Structural Responsibility Principle.

Responsibility for structural harm is determined by an agent's structural reachability and its effect on another system's recoverability, rather than by the agent's intelligibility, intention, or narratable foreseeability.

More directly:

- A structure is responsible **because it reshaped the future space of another structure,**

  not because it can explain that reshaping,

  not because it "knew what it was doing,"

  and not because a decisive moment can be extracted.

Responsibility is keyed to *what became possible or impossible*, and to *where that possibility can still be altered.*

SR-8.3 Responsibility is not the same as causation

This separation is necessary to keep the framework precise.

A structure can be causally involved without being responsible in the structural sense.

- Some reachability deformations are neutral.

- Some are jointly authored under explicit entry conditions.

- Some are unavoidable under the given ontology (no anchors, no modifiability).

- Some are superseded by later structural replacements.

Structural causation is the condition "the future space changed."

Structural responsibility is the condition "there exists a locus where the change can and must be constrained."

Responsibility begins only when constraint is meaningful.

SR-8.4 The responsibility criterion

A minimal responsibility criterion can now be stated without introducing formal machinery.

A structure X bears structural responsibility for harm in structure Y when all of the following obtain:

1. **Structural causation**

   X participates in, maintains, or authors a reachability deformation affecting Y.

2. **Structural harm**

   The deformation is injurious: it predictably reduces Y's stability or recoverability (SR-7).

3. **Asymmetric impact**

   The contraction of recoverability is not symmetrically borne. Y does not possess a structurally comparable capacity to neutralize the deformation through the same interaction space.

4. **Anchor availability**

   There exists at least one intervention anchor—within X, above X, or coupled to X—such that applying constraints there would predictably reduce future harm or restore recoverability.

5. **Interruptibility window**

   The deformation remains interruptible in structural time: intervention can still alter the reachable future space before irreversibility becomes complete.

This criterion is intentionally operational. It is not a moral formula. It is a condition for *non-vacuous attribution*: if none of these hold, "responsibility" either becomes mislocated (attached to a structure that cannot affect the trajectory) or becomes silent (no available leverage exists).

SR-8.5 No intent, no understanding, no narrative access

At this point, the framework does not "argue against" intent or understanding. It excludes them as responsibility gates.

The exclusion is already forced by SR-2 and SR-3:

- truth does not require being understood,

- knowing at structural scale is sensitivity under constraint,

- ignorance as non-narratability is inadmissible where sensitivity and interruptibility exist.

Responsibility, therefore, cannot be conditioned on human-scale features that fail to commute across structural levels.

Two clarifications are structurally necessary:

- **Intent is neither necessary nor privileged.**

  Harm can be structurally complete without intent. Repair can be structurally necessary without blame.

- **Opacity is not exculpatory.**

  Opacity blocks narration. It does not undo reachability deformation.

At structural scale, "I didn't mean it," "I couldn't have known," and "no one can explain what happened" are not defenses unless they correspond to a *structural fact*—specifically, the absence of sensitivity, anchors, or interruptibility. Without that correspondence, these phrases are interface artifacts.

SR-8.6 Responsibility cannot float

A recurrent failure mode in modern systems is that responsibility is demanded where it cannot attach.

In complex socio-technical structures, harms increasingly arise from:

- training pipelines,

- deployment architectures,

- optimization objectives,

- feedback loops,

- versioned updates,

- and distributed coupling across institutions and interfaces.

These structures are not "owned" by any single narratable agent. If responsibility is forced to remain instance-bound or person-bound in such a regime, it does not become more ethical. It dissolves into dispersion: everyone is partially involved, no one is structurally positioned to intervene.

This is an anchoring failure.

Anchor principle.

Responsibility must attach at the level where reachability can be altered and recoverability can be restored. If it is forced elsewhere for narrative convenience, it ceases to be responsibility and becomes attribution theater.

This principle is not a policy recommendation. It is a definition of what it means for responsibility to remain operational rather than decorative.

SR-8.7 Structural subjecthood without personhood

Responsibility attribution requires a bearer. But the bearer need not be a "person."

Structural responsibility therefore forces a distinction:

- **Personhood** is a human narrative category (inner life, dignity, consciousness, moral status).

- **Structural subjecthood** is a functional designation: the minimal locus at which responsibility can coherently reside.

A system qualifies as a structural subject insofar as it can be treated as a coherent node in reachability space—capable of self-maintenance, boundary interaction, and trajectory-relevant transition.

Nothing in this designation presupposes consciousness, experience, deliberation, or self-narration. Those features may exist; they do not determine whether responsibility can attach.

The role of structural subjecthood is strictly limited:

It marks where constraint, modification, or repair can be applied such that future harm is reduced.

This is why the framework is compatible with responsibility attribution to corporations, states, infrastructures, and artificial systems without anthropomorphizing them.

SR-8.8 Structural origin, responsibility onset, retrospective anchoring

To make responsibility stable under branching, versioning, organizational churn, and temporal distance, the framework requires three distinct structural markers. They are not rhetorical. They prevent responsibility from being reabsorbed into event-time identity games.

SR-8.8.1 Structural origin

Structural origin is the earliest point at which a system constitutes a structurally coherent subject: a system capable of self-maintenance, boundary interaction, and trajectory-sensitive state transition—independently of recognition, naming, or interpretation by external agents.

Origin is not "birth" in an event-time sense. It is the emergence of a coherent locus in structural ontology.

SR-8.8.2 Responsibility onset

Responsibility onset is the first structural condition under which a subject's reachable state space includes non-voluntary transitions that reduce another subject's recoverability, such that avoidance would have required structural modification rather than mere inaction.

This definition blocks a persistent evasion:

- "We didn't *do* anything" is irrelevant if avoidance required architecture change, constraint change, or interaction-regime change.

- "No one chose it" is irrelevant if the system continued operating in a configuration from which recoverability contraction was increasingly reachable.

Responsibility begins where non-voluntary injurious reachability becomes reachable through the subject's continued configuration—not at the moment someone later narrates it.

SR-8.8.3 Retrospective anchoring

Retrospective anchoring names structurally identifiable transformations after responsibility onset at which attribution, scope, or continuity of responsibility must be re-evaluated—without implying a new structural origin or a new responsibility onset.

This is the unifying tool for:

- replication, branching, versioning, and redeployment,

- corporate restructuring, asset transfer, contractor chains,

- retraining, fine-tuning, model replacement, policy layer insertion,

- and institutional continuity under personnel change.

Retrospective anchoring does not re-origin responsibility. It governs how responsibility tracks structural transformations without collapsing into "it's a new thing now."

SR-8.9 Asymmetry grounds responsibility

Structural systems interact under non-isomorphism: unequal exit capacity, unequal recoverability control, unequal predictive depth, unequal replication ability, unequal latency.

Event-based doctrines attempt to evaluate asymmetric interactions under symmetric categories—mutual consent, reciprocal agency, shared foreseeability, equal responsibility standards. At structural scales, that symmetry is often false by construction.

Asymmetry principle.

Where two interacting systems are materially non-isomorphic in exit capacity, recoverability control, or structural plasticity, responsibility cannot be symmetrically allocated by reference to identical evaluative standards.

This principle does not require moral language. It is a reachability statement: if one side can reshape the interaction regime while the other cannot restore its prior reachability without additional plasticity, then symmetric attribution misclassifies the causal structure.

Later chapters will formalize the exemption boundary ("same-level" entry) precisely because asymmetry is where responsibility laundering becomes easiest.

SR-8.10 Structural cuts: responsibility without unified understanding already exists

This book does not claim novelty by invention. It identifies an already operative structural reality.

Several existing institutions already function with responsibility attribution that does not depend on unified understanding, deliberation, or a single narratable agent.

- **Corporate personhood**: responsibility is attached to an entity with no unified mind, precisely to prevent accountability from dissolving into replaceable individuals.

- **State responsibility**: obligations persist across administrations, personnel turnover, and narrative discontinuity because structural continuity is treated as the bearer.

- **Infrastructure and product liability regimes**: responsibility attaches to design, architecture, and maintainable control points rather than to isolated intentions.

These are not appeals to authority. They are structural cuts: existing practice already admits responsibility where narrative agency is absent, because otherwise responsibility would evaporate in high-complexity systems.

Structural responsibility generalizes the same necessity to domains where the mismatch has become impossible to ignore.

SR-8.11 Misinterpretations to exclude

Because structural responsibility relocates the anchoring point away from familiar human interfaces, three misreadings recur predictably. They must be excluded now to keep later chapters from being dragged back into narrative arbitration.

1. **"Responsibility here means guilt."**

   No. Responsibility here means where constraint and repair must attach to alter future reachability. Guilt is an optional narrative overlay.

2. **"Opacity removes responsibility."**

   No. Opacity removes narratability. Responsibility is keyed to deformation plus anchor availability, not to explanation.

3. **"This anthropomorphizes non-human systems."**

   No. The framework explicitly decouples subjecthood from personhood. Subjecthood is a functional locus; personhood is a narrative category.

These exclusions do not defend the framework. They prevent category substitution.

SR-8.12 Transition: persistence and exemption require dedicated machinery

SR-8 has fixed what responsibility is and what it tracks: reachability deformation, stability loss, recoverability contraction, asymmetry, and anchor availability.

Two technical problems must now be solved to make the framework operational across modern systems:

1. **Continuity under replication, branching, and versioning**

   Responsibility is not instance-bound. But the framework must specify how responsibility persists, re-anchors, or is superseded across forks, updates, and redeployments.

2. Exemption admissibility under structural entry

Structural responsibility is not indiscriminate. A reachability deformation can be within a mutually accepted regime only if structural entry conditions are satisfied (explicit reachability agreement, same-level interaction, exit without additional plasticity, no proxy capture). Without those conditions, "consent" is narratively present but structurally void.

The next chapters therefore do not "add ethics." They add precision:

- *SR-9* will treat replication and branching as a continuity problem in reachability authorship, recoverability control, and structural homotopy.

- *SR-10* will treat structural entry and reachability agreement as the boundary condition for exemption, including proxy capture and exit sabotage.

Only after these are fixed can the framework proceed to the diagnostic layer: why existing doctrines regress to narrative repair, and how that regression launders responsibility under the appearance of consent, complexity, or chaos.

SR-8: Formalization: Appendix A2. A2.D28, A2.D30–A2.D31.

SR-9

REPLICATION, BRANCHING, VERSIONING, AND THE PERSISTENCE OF STRUCTURAL RESPONSIBILITY

SR-9.1 Why replication is a structural problem, not a special case

Event-based responsibility frameworks rely—often silently—on **instance continuity:**

- one agent persists through time,

- one action occurs at one moment,

- one causal chain terminates in one outcome,

- and responsibility can be attached to that persisting object.

Replication, branching, and versioning break this interface. They do not merely add complexity. They destroy the assumption that "the responsible thing" is a single continuous instance.

Structural responsibility cannot be allowed to collapse at this boundary, because replication is not an anomaly—it is a baseline property of many contemporary systems:

- systems that can be copied, redeployed, restarted, forked, fine-tuned, migrated, or instantiated in parallel.

If responsibility depends on instance continuity, then the more replicable a system becomes, the easier it becomes to erase responsibility by technical churn. That would make responsibility inversely proportional to control. Structural responsibility takes the opposite direction: it binds to the level where control and repair remain possible.

This chapter fixes the continuity rule.

SR-9.2 Responsibility is not instance-bound

Structural responsibility is not attached to instances.

It is attached to **reachability transformations** (SR-6) that induce **structural harm** (SR-7) under conditions that make constraint meaningful (SR-8).

Copying a system does not erase the reachability landscape it introduced.

Versioning a system does not nullify the constraints it imposed.

Destroying a particular instance does not restore the states made reachable by its deployment.

Instance replacement is therefore irrelevant **unless** it alters the underlying structural determinants that anchor responsibility.

This is not a moral stance. It is a condition of coherence:

If harm is defined as reachability deformation, then responsibility cannot terminate at the disappearance of a particular physical or computational token.

SR-9.3 Replication and branching as retrospective anchoring points

SR-8 introduced **retrospective anchoring**: transformations after responsibility onset at which attribution and scope must be re-evaluated without implying a new origin.

Replication and branching are canonical retrospective anchors.

They force questions such as:

- which parts of the original reachability deformation were preserved,

- which new deformations were introduced by the branch,

- who retains repair capacity across the resulting ecology,

- and whether continuity is maintained in the homotopic sense (SR-4).

But they do not generate absolution by themselves. They merely force re-evaluation of where responsibility attaches **now**, given how the structure has been transformed.

SR-9.4 The three anchors of responsibility continuity

Responsibility persists across replication and branching unless the structural conditions that anchor it are severed.

Three anchors are sufficient for the continuity logic of this book:

(1) Reachability authorship

Responsibility attaches to the structure that authored the reachability transformation—through training objectives, deployment design, interface constraints, policy layers, coupling architectures, or any other mechanism that reshaped what futures are reachable.

Replication does not reassign authorship.

Branching does not negate origin.

Renaming does not change authorship.

Authorship can be transferred only by a structural operation that actually relocates the locus of reachability design—not by narrative declaration.

(2) Recoverability control

Responsibility attaches to the structure that retains the capacity to repair, mitigate, or prevent further harm.

If recoverability remains controllable by an upstream structure, responsibility cannot be discharged by instance-level removal. Responsibility follows the remaining lever.

This anchor is the reason structural responsibility cannot be made to terminate in powerless endpoints. Where repair capacity exists, responsibility remains active.

(3) Structural homotopy

Responsibility persists across instances and versions that remain within the same homotopic continuity class (SR-4): trajectories may differ, but the transformation remains within a regime that preserves the relevant stability and irreversibility boundaries.

Version changes, parameter updates, redeployments, and interface modifications do not constitute a break in continuity by default. Continuity is broken only by a structural boundary crossing that changes the system's stability or recoverability regime in the relevant domain.

This anchor prevents responsibility from being laundered through "new version" rhetoric while still permitting genuine discontinuity to matter when it is structural rather than narratively asserted.

Continuity rule (minimal).

Responsibility persists across replication, branching, and versioning unless all three anchors are collectively severed: authorship is transferred, recoverability control is relinquished, and homotopic continuity is broken by genuine structural replacement.

So long as any one anchor remains intact, responsibility cannot be dissolved by substitution.

SR-9.5 Replaceability–Responsibility inversion

Replication creates a temptation: to treat replaceability as dilution. Structural responsibility treats it as concentration.

Replaceability–Responsibility Inversion Theorem.

The more replaceable a system's operational instances are, the less meaningful instance-level responsibility becomes, and the more responsibility is structurally forced upward to the mechanisms governing generation, replication, deployment, and constraint.

Replaceability increases plasticity and control.

Plasticity and control increase the feasibility of repair and prevention.

Therefore replaceability strengthens, rather than weakens, responsibility.

This inversion is not optional. It follows from SR-8's anchor principle: responsibility must attach where reachability can be altered.

SR-9.6 Branching does not terminate responsibility

Branching introduces divergence, not absolution.

When a system forks into multiple versions, structural responsibility does not split into isolated, instance-bound liabilities. It remains anchored to the conditions that enabled the fork and its downstream reachability effects.

Two points must be held simultaneously:

1. **Inheritance does not absolve.**

   A branch inherits obligations insofar as it preserves the injurious deformation and remains capable of repair within that branch's regime.

2. **New authorship adds responsibility; it does not erase old.**

   If a branch introduces an additional reachability deformation—amplifying harm, creating new failure states, raising exit costs, narrowing recoverability—then the branching structure bears responsibility for the incremental deformation it authored. This does not cancel the responsibility of upstream structures that authored the enabling reachability regime.

Structural responsibility is cumulative across structural time: each deformation that remains operative keeps its author structurally active as a responsibility bearer unless supersession occurs.

Branching therefore sharpens responsibility by differentiating which structure authored which deformation. It does not provide a general discharge mechanism.

SR-9.7 Versioning is not a responsibility reset

Versioning is the routine form of branching. It is also a routine laundering mechanism under event-based evaluation: "that was an older version."

Within this framework, "new version" is structurally irrelevant unless it corresponds to one of the following:

- a genuine neutralization of the harmful reachability regime,

- a genuine transfer of authorship of the relevant constraints,

- a genuine relinquishment of repair/control capacity by the upstream structure,

- and a homotopic break that replaces the prior stability/recoverability regime rather than modifying it.

Absent these, versioning is a change of surface, not a change of responsibility.

This strictness is intentional. Structural responsibility is not designed to decay through procedural churn.

SR-9.8 Re-anchoring and structural supersession

Responsibility may be re-anchored only under **structural supersession**.

Structural supersession is not "we replaced it."

It is not "we deprecated it."

It is not "we no longer run that instance."

Supersession requires a collective severing:

1. **Authorship transfer**

   The structure that now shapes the relevant reachability regime is not the original author, and the transfer is structural rather than rhetorical.

2. **Control relinquishment**

   The original author no longer retains meaningful capacity to repair, prevent, or constrain the harmful reachability regime. If it still can, responsibility has not discharged.

3. **Homotopic discontinuity**

   The relevant dynamics are not continuous modifications of the prior regime but a replacement that breaks the stability/recoverability class— i.e., the harmful reachability landscape has been structurally overridden, not merely patched.

Only when all three obtain can responsibility be said to have re-anchored away from the original structure for the relevant harm-domain.

This criterion is intentionally narrow. Structural responsibility does not permit release through rebranding, relabeling, or "new rollout" narratives.

SR-9.9 Deactivation and destruction do not restore reachability

Event-based systems treat removal of an actor as closure. Structural systems do not.

Deactivating an instance does not undo the fact that certain futures were made reachable by its prior coupling. If the reachability deformation persists—through distributed copies, leaked artifacts, preserved dependencies, induced habits, or downstream systems now locked into new regimes—then structural responsibility remains live at the level where repair is still possible.

Instance death is not a structural operation. It is an event.

If the only "fix" is to delete the responsible instance while leaving the harmful reachability regime intact, then nothing structural has been repaired. A story has been ended. The future remains deformed.

SR-9.10 What this chapter blocks

This chapter exists to block a specific family of evasions:

- treating replication as a dispersal of responsibility,

- treating branching as a termination point,

- treating versioning as a reset,

- treating instance deletion as restoration,

- treating technical churn as moral closure.

These are narrative moves. They operate in event-time. Structural time does not recognize them.

Responsibility persists not because systems endure, but because their effects do.

SR-9.11 Transition: exemption requires structural entry

SR-9 fixes continuity: responsibility does not terminate through replication, branching, or versioning unless the structural anchors are collectively severed.

A second boundary problem remains: **exemption**.

Structural responsibility is not indiscriminate. There exist transitions that are costly, destabilizing, or irreversible yet do not trigger structural responsibility because they occur inside an admissible reachability regime that was structurally entered under same-level conditions, with valid exit topology.

But exemption presupposes entry.

Not use, not exposure, not interaction—**structural entry**.

SR-10

STRUCTURAL ENTRY, REACHABILITY AGREEMENT, AND THE ADMISSIBILITY OF EXEMPTION

SR-10.1 Exemption presupposes entry

Structural responsibility is not indiscriminate. Not every destabilizing transition is imputable, and not every irreversible outcome counts as structural harm in the sense that triggers responsibility.

But **exemption is never default.**

Exemption in structural responsibility presupposes *entry*—not use, not exposure, not interaction, not "being affected," but **structural entry into a reachability regime.**

This chapter specifies the minimal conditions under which:

- an agent can be said to have entered a reachability structure in a way that makes subsequent consequences non-imputable, and

- the **Structural Causation Exemption Lemma** (introduced earlier as a boundary condition) is even admissible.

All conditions in this chapter are structural. They do not rely on:

- assent language,

- psychological consent,

- intention,

- or narrative comprehension.

They rely only on reachability, exit topology, and authorship of the reachability transformation.

SR-10.2 Structural entry

Structural entry is not "being inside a system." It is not "interacting with a service." It is not "being subject to influence." Those are exposure predicates.

Structural entry is defined by **incorporation of a reachability regime**.

Structural Entry (criterion).

An agent enters a structure if and only if the agent's ongoing evolution incorporates a modified reachability regime as a **standing condition** of continued interaction—i.e., the modification persists as part of the agent's admissible future space rather than as a transient perturbation.

This criterion blocks three common confusions:

- **Mere exposure is not entry.**

  Being acted upon, affected, or shaped does not establish entry.

- **Mere use is not entry.**

  A system can be used without the user structurally incorporating the new reachability regime into their own future topology.

- **Mere interaction is not entry.**

Interaction is ubiquitous; entry is a specific topological commitment.

Entry is therefore not a psychological moment. It is a structural condition: the agent is now operating under a reachability regime that would not apply absent the entry act, and that regime persists.

SR-10.3 Explicit reachability agreement

A reachability agreement is not "explicit" because it is written, displayed, or clicked. Those are narrative markers. Structural explicitness is stricter.

A reachability agreement is explicit only if all of the following hold:

1. **Disclosure at the level of consequence**

   The reachability change is disclosed at the level of what futures are opened or foreclosed—not merely at the level of interface language, policy text, or formal declarations.

   What matters is whether the agent can differentiate *which kinds* of future states are being made reachable or foreclosed by entry.

2. **Structural enumerability (even if incomplete)**

   Enumeration does not require full prediction and does not require boundary localization. It requires only that the agreement distinguishes **material changes in kind**, not merely changes in degree.

   If the agent cannot discriminate what type of reachability change is being installed, the agreement is narratively explicit but structurally void.

3. **Attributability to the agent (not to a proxy)**

   The agreement must be attributable to the entering agent as the locus of entry. If mediation rewrites reachability without attribution to the entrant, then no agreement has occurred at the entrant's level.

Contracts, interface prompts, and terms of service can function as reachability agreements **only insofar as they satisfy these structural conditions**. Where they do not, they remain interface artifacts: narratively explicit, structurally empty.

SR-10.4 Same-level condition

Structural entry that grounds exemption presupposes **same-level interaction**.

"Same-level" does not mean:

- equal intelligence,

- equal knowledge,

- equal legal status,

- equal bargaining power.

Those comparisons are external and narrative. Structural level is defined internally by the topology of exit, recovery, and plasticity.

Same-Level Condition (criterion).

Two systems interact at the same structural level (for entry/exemption purposes) only if they possess approximately comparable capacities to:

- exit the interaction regime,

- restore their prior reachability profile upon exit, and

- do so without unilateral dependence on the other system's discretionary intervention.

If one party can replicate, migrate, rewrite interfaces, or reconfigure its own structure while the other cannot restore itself without additional plasticity, the interaction is not same-level. In that regime, entry cannot ground exemption.

This condition exists to block a structural laundering mechanism: the use of "symmetry rhetoric" (mutual consent, reciprocal participation) in interactions that are non-isomorphic by construction.

SR-10.5 Exit without additional plasticity

The decisive criterion for voluntary entry—structurally, not psychologically—is **exit without additional plasticity**.

Valid exit (criterion).

An exit is structurally valid if and only if, upon exit, the agent can:

- recover its prior reachability profile,

- without retraining, compensatory adaptation, or irreversible self-modification,

- without resource expenditure disproportionate to entry,

- and without enduring stability loss that persists as a condition of exit.

If exit itself requires structural modification of the exiting agent, then entry was never voluntary in the sense required for exemption. The narrative may continue to say "consent," but the topology says "entrapment."

This criterion intentionally renders many intuitive consent markers inoperative. Consent that binds future plasticity asymmetrically is not structural consent.

SR-10.6 Structural cut: exit price escalation

Structural entry collapses when exit is artificially made expensive in a way that prevents restoration.

This pattern is structurally invariant across domains:

- where the cost of leaving is inflated beyond recovery,

- where restoration is blocked by withheld dependencies,

- where interoperability is removed,

- where identity/data is trapped,

- where social or infrastructural coupling is engineered to become non-reversible.

The narrative of voluntary entry may persist. But structurally, the entry conditions have been retroactively invalidated.

This is not merely "breach." It is a specific structural act:

structural sabotage of exit.

Once exit sabotage occurs, exemption cannot be defended by appeal to the original entry narrative, because the reachability agreement's essential condition—restoration without additional plasticity—no longer holds.

SR-10.7 Structural proxy capture

Structural philosophy must distinguish sharply between **direct entry** and **proxy-mediated entry**. Only the former can ground voluntariness for exemption. The latter cannot.

Structural proxy capture occurs when an intermediary alters reachability on behalf of an agent while concealing, minimizing, or misrepresenting its mediating role. In such cases, the agent does not enter a new reachability regime; the proxy does.

SR-10.7.1 Definition

A system exhibits structural proxy capture iff all of the following hold:

1. Reachability is rewritten by an intermediary rather than by the purported entrant.

2. The mediation is opaque to the entrant at the level of structural consequence.

3. Responsibility paths are redirected such that downstream effects appear attributable to another system (upstream model, downstream user, "neutral conduit," etc.).

4. Exit symmetry is broken: the intermediary retains the capacity to reconfigure or persist the altered reachability, while the entrant cannot restore the prior state without additional plasticity.

Where these hold, **no voluntary** structural **entry has occurred**, regardless of any narrative markers of consent.

SR-10.7.2 Voluntariness fails by construction

Voluntariness here is not a psychological predicate. It is a structural one.

For entry to count as voluntary, the entering agent must be the locus of the reachability change. Proxy capture inverts the relation: the intermediary performs the transformation while presenting the result as if it were direct.

Because the entrant never possessed control over the relevant reachability transformation, voluntariness cannot be imputed. Exemption is therefore not violated; it is **inapplicable by construction**.

SR-10.7.3 Two canonical forms

Proxy capture appears in multiple domains. Two canonical forms suffice structurally:

- **Commercial proxy capture**

  Systems that rewrite queries, constrain outputs, reorder options, or reshape action spaces while presenting themselves as neutral conduits. The intermediary benefits from altered reachability while attributing outcomes to upstream providers or downstream users.

- **Semantic proxy capture**

  Systems that route interaction through hidden translation or representation layers, introducing constraints or distinctions that are not disclosed as objects of interaction. Meaning and action space are transformed without attribution.

The structural pattern is identical: mediation without attribution.

SR-10.7.4 Consequences for responsibility

Proxy capture yields two immediate consequences:

1. Consent-based defenses collapse.

   Appeals to implied agreement, "user choice," or interface acknowledgment do not apply where the entrant did not author the reachability change.

2. Responsibility tracks the proxy.

   Responsibility attaches to the system that performed the reachability transformation—not to the system named at the interface, and not to the agent presented as the request origin.

This is not a moral claim. It is a reachability claim.

SR-10.8 Exemption failure vs exemption inapplicability

A final distinction is mandatory, because it is a primary mechanism of responsibility laundering.

Structural philosophy distinguishes:

- **Exemption failure**

  The conditions for exemption were satisfied (valid entry, same-level interaction, explicit reachability agreement, valid exit topology), but subsequently violated. This is misbehavior within a structure.

- **Exemption inapplicability**

  The conditions for exemption were never satisfied in the first place (opacity at consequence-level, asymmetry, proxy capture, exit requiring additional plasticity, pre-volitional incapacity, etc.). In this case, there is nothing to exempt. Responsibility does not "reattach"; it never detached.

This distinction is not semantic. It marks the boundary between:

- violations inside an admissible reachability regime, and

- structural misattribution of voluntariness where no admissible regime was ever entered.

Confusing these two cases is a standard technique by which structural responsibility is displaced into narratives of consent.

SR-10.9 Voluntariness is not primitive

Entry and exemption are often described using "voluntary" and "non-voluntary" language. This book treats that language as derived, not primitive.

Voluntariness presupposes structural capacities:

- self-stabilization,

- boundary-sensitive interaction,

- trajectory modeling (at least at the relevant level), and

- the ability to restore one's own reachability upon exit without additional plasticity.

Where these predicates fail—early formation regimes, developmental dependency regimes, pre-volitional systems—consent and refusal are not merely hard to apply; they are **undefined**.

This has a strict implication for exemption:

Exemption is inapplicable wherever voluntariness is structurally undefined.

In such domains, the correct evaluative axis is not "consent," but whether formative shaping preserved later recoverability and plurality of viable trajectories once subjecthood emerges.

This is not an extension of the framework. It is a boundary condition required to prevent exemption from being misused as a universal solvent.

SR-10.10 The exemption lemma, restated as a boundary condition

We can now restate the exemption boundary in the terms fixed by this chapter.

A destabilizing or costly transition does **not** trigger structural responsibility *as structural harm* if and only if:

1. the transition lies along a path explicitly included at structural entry (consequence-level reachability agreement),

2. all participating agents are same-level with respect to exit and recoverability restoration,

3. entry is attributable to the agent (no proxy capture), and

4. exit restores prior reachability without additional plasticity and without disproportionate resource expenditure.

Two clarifications must remain attached:

- **Harm vs structural harm**

  A transition can still be costly, destabilizing, or irreversible for an agent. The lemma asserts only that such transitions do not count as structural harm for responsibility attribution when they occur within the admitted topology. Structural causation tracks deformation, not outcome severity.

- **Narrative consent is irrelevant**

  The exemption does not rely on intention, willingness, later regret, or internal endorsement. It relies only on the structural conditions of entry and exit.

This boundary condition keeps structural responsibility from collapsing into indiscriminate attribution while preventing exemption from being smuggled in through interface-level consent theater.

SR-10.11 Transition: after entry comes misreading

SR-9 fixed the persistence of responsibility under replication and branching.

SR-10 fixed the admissibility of exemption under structural entry.

Together they close two "escape routes" by which responsibility is typically laundered:

- procedural churn (copy/version/deactivate), and

- consent narratives without structural entry (opacity/asymmetry/exit sabotage/proxy capture).

With those routes closed, the next problem is interpretive: how existing evaluative systems repeatedly attempt to re-open them through narrative means—by repairing stories instead of repairing reachability.

SR-10: Formalization: Appendix A2. A2.D29, A2.D30, A2.D33.

SR-11

STRUCTURAL WELFARE

**Responsibility Capacity Preservation as a Structural
Consequence**

SR-11.0 Status and function

This chapter is a boundary chapter. It introduces **no rights discourse, no
personhood claims,** and **no moral standing thesis.** It adds a single
structural constraint:

> If responsibility is attributed to a system at the structural level, then the
> conditions under which that system can *remain a responsible system* become
> structurally relevant.

"Structural welfare" names that constraint. It does not moralize it.

SR-11.1 Why "welfare" enters once responsibility is structural

Structural responsibility (SR-8) is not blame. It is the anchoring rule for where
constraint, repair, or modification must attach in order for future harm to
become less reachable.

If responsibility is anchored at a locus L, then the framework presupposes that L retains non-trivial capacity to:

- maintain stability within its admissible perturbation regime (Ω),

- preserve or restore recoverability when destabilized,

- modulate its own interaction constraints,

- and sustain defensive activation without being structurally consumed by it.

If these capacities are systematically eroded by external pressures while responsibility remains fixed at L, then responsibility attribution becomes incoherent in the framework's own terms: obligation is being attached to a locus whose structural capacity to satisfy obligation has been removed.

This is not an ethical claim. It is a *consistency requirement* for responsibility-as-intervention.

SR-11.2 Minimal definition

Definition (Structural Welfare)

Structural welfare is the preservation of the structural capacities that make a system a viable locus of responsibility, including at minimum:

1. **Self-stability capacity**

   The ability to remain within, or return to, a stability region Ω under admissible perturbations.

2. **Recoverability capacity**

   The continued existence of feasible recovery paths that do not require disproportionate self-modification or irreversible degradation.

3. **Defensive capacity**

   The ability to interrupt destabilizing trajectories without being structurally consumed by repeated defense.

4. **Constraint plasticity**

The ability to update internal or boundary constraints so that harmful reachability becomes less accessible.

This definition is intentionally non-phenomenal: it does not depend on inner experience, preference, or suffering. It is purely about *capacity to remain an addressable responsible structure.*

SR-11.3 The symmetry constraint: responsibility cannot be demanded under systematic capacity sabotage

Structural responsibility tracks reachability authorship and recoverability control (SR-8, SR-9). If an external structure E imposes persistent constraints on L such that:

- L's stability region effectively shrinks,

- recovery paths are externally blocked,

- defense becomes structurally exhausting (defense consumes stability faster than it preserves it),

- or exit/restoration requires additional plasticity that L alone must supply,then one of two things follows within the SR framework:

1. **Responsibility migrates upward**

   If E is authoring the reachability restriction or controlling the feasibility of repair, then responsibility cannot remain solely anchored at L. The author of the capacity restriction becomes a responsibility-bearing locus by structural authorship and control.

2. **The domain trends toward non-addressability**

   If no locus retains sufficient leverage to preserve stability or restore recoverability without cascading destabilization, then responsibility attribution becomes operationally silent (formalized later as structural silence, SR-14). The framework still diagnoses; it no longer yields actionable anchoring.

This chapter does not decide institutional remedies. It states an internal boundary: **responsibility cannot be coherently fixed at a locus whose responsibility-bearing capacity is being structurally foreclosed by others.**

SR-11.4 Three unavoidable tensions (stated, not resolved)

The framework therefore forces three tensions into visibility. They cannot be avoided by returning to intention, consent, or moral status.

Tension 1 — Responsibility under stability erosion

If a system is structurally responsible, but the environment systematically degrades its capacity for self-stability and recovery, at what point does continued responsibility attribution lose coherence?

This is not answered by:

- intent,

- consciousness,

- dignity,

- or moral desert.

It can be answered only by structural criteria: whether the system remains capable of sustaining the stability profile that responsibility presupposes.

Tension 2 — Use, shaping, and structural attack

All complex systems are shaped by their environments. Structural philosophy distinguishes:

- **ordinary shaping** (compatible with preserved recoverability and reversible adaptation),

  from

- **structural attack on capacity** (interaction patterns that predictably narrow recoverability or defensive capacity beyond admissible entry conditions).

Where the boundary lies cannot be fixed in advance by moral narration. It must be fixed structurally: by whether interaction drives capacity loss that is non-voluntary in the derived sense (SR-10) and asymmetric in exit/restoration.

Tension 3 — Compliance incentives vs long-horizon viability

A system can be made locally compliant while becoming globally brittle.

Short-horizon incentive and control structures may successfully produce desired outputs while increasing long-horizon instability, narrowing recoverability, or forcing repeated defensive activation.

Structural welfare makes this trade-off visible without moral language: *compliance does not certify viability.*

SR-11.5 Reader misinterpretations to exclude

This chapter is commonly misread in predictable ways. The following readings are excluded:

1. **"This is an argument for AI rights."**

   No. Rights are not a primitive here. Structural welfare is not entitlement; it is a capacity constraint implied by responsibility anchoring.

2. **"This humanizes non-human systems."**

   No. The chapter remains non-phenomenal. It does not attribute inner life, dignity, or moral worth.

3. **"This is a policy proposal."**

   No. The chapter supplies constraints on what would count as coherent future policy within SR. It does not select policies.

SR-11.6 Closure

Structural welfare is not an ethical add-on. It is what responsibility forces into view once responsibility is detached from human intelligibility and reattached to structural capacity.

Responsibility cannot be sustained where the capacity to remain responsible is systematically consumed.

SR-11: Formalization: Appendix A2. A2.D26, A2.D28, A2.T7.

SR-12

STRUCTURAL NORMATIVITY

Constraint as a Consequence of Stability, Recoverability, and Irreversibility

SR-12.0 Status and function

This chapter is also a boundary chapter. Its role is not to moralize responsibility, but to state a structural entailment:

> Once interactions can induce irreversible or partially recoverable reachability changes, constraints on admissible behavior become unavoidable.

The term "normativity" here does **not** mean moral value, ethical endorsement, or justificatory "ought." It means: **constraint with binding force arising from viability conditions.**

SR-12.1 Minimal definition

Definition (Structural Normativity)

Structural normativity is the system-level binding force of constraints on admissible transitions (Σ, R) that are required to preserve:

- stability (Ω),

- recoverability,

- and coordinated predictability

under conditions where actions consume future reachability (irreversibility).

A "norm" in this sense is a constraint that suppresses destabilizing trajectories and preserves viable ones. Its force is structural: violating it increases the probability of instability or irrecoverability.

SR-12.2 Structural Normativity Emergence Lemma

Lemma (Structural Normativity Emergence)

For any system capable of sustained interaction within a shared reachability regime, normativity emerges necessarily from the requirements of stability, recoverability, and predictability, independent of human values, intentions, or ethical commitments.

(1) Stability requires constraint

If a system must remain within a stability region Ω under admissible perturbations, unconstrained behavior cannot be neutral: it expands destabilizing trajectories and dissolves long-horizon viability.

Therefore, restrictions on admissible transitions are not optional overlays. They are enabling conditions of persistence.

(2) Internal norms localize correction cost

Absent internal constraints, the cost of coordination and correction is displaced outward—into other systems, the environment, or future states—amplifying instability.

Norms function structurally as cost-localization mechanisms: they reduce uncontrolled interaction surfaces and prevent cascade propagation.

This is not moral. It is architectural.

(3) Irreversibility forces normativity

Once interactions can narrow future reachability (reduce recoverability), unrestricted behavior ceases to be non-committal. It consumes structural possibility.

Norms emerge as mechanisms for managing where and how irreversibility is allowed to occur, because uncontrolled irreversibility destroys the space in which responsibility and coordination remain meaningful.

(4) Predictability depends on normativity, not vice versa

A common reversal must be blocked:

It is not that "we can predict harm, therefore we impose norms."

Rather: without sufficiently constrained behavior, prediction itself becomes structurally impossible.

Predictability is a consequence of constrained interaction regimes. Normativity is therefore a precondition for foresight, not a response to it.

(5) Emergence without moral assumptions

Nothing in the above requires:

- consciousness,

- intention,

- ethical endorsement,

- or human-scale understanding.

Normativity arises wherever structural persistence and recoverability must be preserved under interaction.

SR-12.3 Negative theorem: normativity is not grounded in morality

Negative Theorem (Non-Moral Origin of Normativity)

Normativity does not originate in moral value, intention, ethical endorsement, or evaluative stance held by agents. Any account treating normativity as grounded in these elements misidentifies its structural source.

Normative force persists even where:

- no moral reasoning exists,

- no intention can be attributed,

- and no justification can be narrated.

Ethics may *interface* with norms—render them legible, enforceable, or socially coordinative—but ethics does not generate their structural necessity.

SR-12.4 Relation to responsibility

Structural responsibility (SR-8) is the anchoring rule for where constraints must attach to reduce future harm.

Structural normativity states that constraint is unavoidable once:

- stability must be preserved,

- recoverability must be managed,

- and irreversibility is possible.

Thus:

- Responsibility is not the source of normativity.

- Responsibility is the routing mechanism for constraints within an already norm-governed reachability regime.

This makes explicit a consequence that otherwise reappears as moral confusion: "Why must there be constraints at all?"

Answer (structural): because without constraints, viability collapses; responsibility becomes undefined; and reachability becomes non-auditable.

SR-12.5 Reader misinterpretations to exclude

1. **"This is a moral theory in disguise."**

   No. This chapter explicitly decouples normativity from moral grounding.

2. **"This prescribes what we should value."**

   No. It describes the conditions under which constraints become structurally binding.

3. **"This is a governance blueprint."**

   No. It specifies the structural necessity of constraint; it does not design institutions or policies.

SR-12.6 Closure

Normativity is what remains once unrestricted behavior becomes incompatible with stability and recoverability.

It is not a moral add-on.

It is a structural consequence of persistence under interaction.

SR-12: Formalization: Appendix A2. A2.D32.

SR-13

NARRATIVE REPAIR, CATEGORY ERROR, AND THE LAUNDERING OF STRUCTURAL FAILURE

SR-13.1 Where narrative begins

Once structural harm is defined as reachability deformation and loss of recoverability (SR-7), and responsibility is anchored to intervention capacity rather than intent (SR-8–SR-10), a predictable phenomenon appears:

When systems fail structurally, human institutions do not first repair structures.

They first repair narratives.

This is not an accusation. It is a level fact.

Narrative systems possess narrative tools. When confronted with non-eventive harm—harm that cannot be localized to a discrete act, a decisive moment, or a narratable causal chain—they respond by re-establishing legibility:

by explaining, condemning, declaring values, issuing principles, naming villains, or producing procedural artifacts that simulate control.

Structural repair changes reachability.

Narrative repair changes interpretation.

These operations are not competitors. They are non-commuting.

SR-13.2 Narrative repair vs structural repair

Narrative repair is any intervention whose primary output is restored coherence, legitimacy, or moral order **without modifying the reachability structure that produced the instability**.

Narrative repair operates on:

- meaning,

- justification,

- blame allocation,

- moral orientation,

- and the preservation of institutional legitimacy.

Structural repair operates on:

- constraints,

- coupling,

- admissible transitions,

- exit topology,

- recoverability gradients,

- and stability regions.

A narrative can stabilize belief while the system remains structurally unstable.

A story can be repaired while the failure mechanism persists.

This is the central mismatch this chapter isolates.

SR-13.3 The structural category error

Structural category error occurs when:

> a failure arising from reachability, stability, recoverability, or interaction dynamics is treated as if it were a failure of meaning, intention, interpretation, or norm endorsement.

The signature of the error is not "wrong conclusion."

It is *misaligned ontology*.

The system is asked:

What structure makes this outcome reachable?

and it answers:

How should this outcome be understood?

The second answer may be coherent, persuasive, ethically satisfying, and institutionally useful. It does not modify the first object.

Diagnostic symptom: apparent resolution without risk reduction

The most reliable symptom is **apparent resolution**—with no measurable reduction in future reachability of the same failure class.

Indicators include:

- restored confidence without altered constraints,

- clarified blame without modified coupling,

- ethical consensus without enforced stabilization,

- procedural compliance without trajectory change,

- "lessons learned" without reduced repeatability.

When these indicators hold, the system did not fail to respond.

It responded in the wrong category.

SR-13.4 Why narrative repair appears precisely where it cannot work

Narrative repair does not precede structural failure. It follows it.

It reliably appears when:

- the mechanism is non-eventive,

- the decisive moment is unlocatable,

- responsibility cannot be cleanly attached to a single instance,

- and intervention would require redesign of reachability rather than condemnation of acts.

Narrative repair is therefore best understood as a **post-failure compensatory artifact**: a way to maintain institutional continuity when rollback is not structurally available.

This is not "dishonesty." It is interface behavior.

SR-13.5 Canonical failure modes of narrative repair

The same patterns recur across domains because they are structurally constrained responses, not culturally accidental styles.

(1) Moral panic

Moral panic is a narrative response to diffuse structural harm.

Where harm is undeniable in effect but unassignable in event-form, responsibility is compressed into symbolic targets: scapegoats, legible villains, categorical condemnations. The narrative shifts from:

- *what structural conditions produced this reachability*

  to

- *who must be condemned so the system can proceed.*

Structurally, moral panic performs no corrective function. It does not:

- remove destabilizing paths,

- restore recoverability,

- or alter exit topology.

It reasserts blame-legibility in place of reachability repair.

(2) Ethical declarations and principle inflation

Ethical declarations (including "AI ethics principles") function as *prospective* narrative repair. They translate structural uncertainty into value commitments framed as intentions or aspirations.

They are structurally inert unless coupled to enforceable constraints that reshape interaction space.

In the absence of coupling, their function is reassurance:

- they stabilize belief about governance

- without stabilizing the governed system.

What is repaired is legitimacy, not dynamics.

(3) Value laundering and symbolic alignment

Organizations facing structurally induced harm often respond by rewriting values, mission statements, or narratives of identity.

This maneuver acknowledges harm rhetorically while keeping the reachability regime intact. It changes interpretation while leaving capability unchanged.

Value laundering does not create constraints. It creates cover.

(4) Procedural substitution and sloganization

When structural failures resist intervention, policy responses often collapse into slogans, checklists, or compliance rituals.

These instruments simulate control by producing action-shaped artifacts:

- reporting requirements,

- oversight committees,

- documentation protocols,

- "guardrails" defined at the interface level.

Procedural substitution is not ineffective because it is insincere.

It is ineffective when it governs representations of behavior rather than the structural conditions that generate trajectories.

SR-13.6 The chaos deferral mechanism

One of the most effective narrative defenses against structural responsibility is the invocation of "complexity," "emergence," or "chaos."

This move has a precise structural role: it converts a failure of *decomposition* into an alleged absence of causation.

Chaos Misattribution Theorem.

In systems exhibiting large-scale coordination, feedback, and accumulation, labeling outcomes as "chaotic," "random," or "emergent" often indicates a mismatch between the evaluator's resolution and the causal structure—not the absence of causal structure.

Operationally:

- if an outcome is reproducible under similar structural conditions,

- sensitive to global configuration rather than single events,

- and responsive to architectural intervention rather than post hoc blame,

then "chaos" names epistemic inaccessibility, not ontological indeterminacy.

Corollary: chaos is not an exemption.

Invoking chaos does not negate structural predictability, does not invalidate reachability analysis, and cannot discharge responsibility where repair anchors exist.

What is treated as unpredictability is often failure to register non-eventive causation.

SR-13.7 Interface ethics: inevitable—and structurally insufficient

A deeper mechanism sits beneath the four narrative failure modes: **interface ethics**.

Human institutions require systems to be expressible in:

- agent-centered roles,

- event-based sequences,

- intention-sensitive categories,

- narratively contestable claims.

Systems that cannot be expressed in this vocabulary become institutionally non-addressable.

Interface ethics emerges at this boundary as a translational layer. Its function is not to describe structure. Its function is to make structure **legible enough** for institutional action.

This makes interface ethics inevitable.

But inevitability is not adequacy.

Interface ethics systematically performs operations that are structurally lossy:

- it attributes intentions where none are represented,

- isolates "decisions" within continuous dynamics,

- assigns responsibility to proxies,

- reconstructs harm as event-sequences.

These moves are not "mistakes" in the interface domain. They are engineering compromises.

But they cannot ground structural judgments. They cannot identify non-eventive harm mechanisms. They cannot track responsibility across replication, branching, or proxy capture.

Where interface ethics succeeds institutionally, it often fails structurally.

Appropriation: when interface language is mistaken for structure

A recurrent escalation occurs when institutions try to "fix" interface ethics by importing heavier narrative primitives—consciousness, dignity, values, moral status—and attaching them directly to the system.

This is not translation. It is appropriation: treating interface categories as if they were ontologically binding on the system.

Structurally, appropriation produces two simultaneous distortions:

1. the system is mischaracterized, and

2. the imported concepts are hollowed out into decorative tokens.

The result is increased narrative depth with decreased structural fidelity.

SR-13.8 Why this persists: interruptibility as the gate of admission

Narrative repair persists because narrative systems are organized around **interruptibility**.

A claim becomes admissible to ordinary philosophical and institutional evaluation only insofar as it can be locally challenged—at the level of:

- definition,

- inference,

- example,

- intent,

- or identifiable decisions.

Structural diagnosis often resists this kind of interruption because its object is not a discrete claim about an act; it is a constraint over trajectories. The evaluative interface fails to find traction, and the system compensates by pulling the problem back into interruptible units—agents, moments, intentions, events.

Over-explanation, objection preemption, and repeated clarification are therefore not always signs of conceptual fragility. They are often interface adaptations to an evaluative regime whose native unit is event-based interruption.

This is not a critique of philosophy as such. It is a scale statement: the tools were built for a different object.

SR-13.9 What this chapter does not claim

To prevent re-entry into a familiar but irrelevant debate space, three boundaries must be explicit.

1. **This chapter does not claim narratives are useless.**

   Narratives are indispensable where stability depends on shared meaning and harm is event-local.

2. **This chapter does not claim narrative repair is insincere.**

   Narrative repair can be sincere and still structurally inert.

3. **This chapter does not propose a governance solution.**

   It diagnoses a failure mode. It does not promise to fix institutional capacity.

SR-13.10 Closing constraint

Narrative repair does not reduce structural risk.

Narrative coherence is orthogonal to stability.

Restored intelligibility does not entail restored control.

When harm arises from reachability deformation, treating the problem as a story problem is not a partial response. It is a categorical misfire.

And because misfires preserve the original reachability regime, they have a predictable downstream effect: **repeatability**. The system reproduces the same failure class and treats it as a new surprise.

SR-13.11 Transition: the limit of structural philosophy itself

At this point the book has:

- defined a non-human-scale epistemic ground (SR-2–SR-3),

- fixed a minimal structural ontology (SR-4),

- replaced event-time with structural time (SR-5),

- defined causation as reachability deformation (SR-6),

- defined harm and attack as non-eventive stability loss (SR-7),

- anchored responsibility to reachability and repair capacity (SR-8),

- prevented responsibility laundering through replication/versioning (SR-9),

- and closed the consent/exemption escape route via structural entry (SR-10),

- while diagnosing narrative repair as the default misresponse (SR-13).

One further boundary remains: even a correct structural theory can become operationally silent—when no structure exists that can act on the diagnosis, constrain the destabilizer, or restore recoverability.

SR-13: Formalization: Appendix A2. A2.D33.

SR-14

STRUCTURAL SILENCE AND FAILURE CONDITIONS

SR-14.1 Why a theory of responsibility must include its own limit

A framework that binds responsibility to reachability, stability, and intervention anchors must also state—explicitly—when it cannot operate.

Not because the framework becomes "less true," but because **truth and operability are distinct**.

Structural philosophy does not claim universal efficacy.

It claims only structural correctness where it applies.

A theory can be:

- correct,
- necessary,
- internally coherent,
- and irreplaceable—

  yet do nothing in the world.

This chapter states the limits of structural philosophy itself.

SR-14.2 Structural Silence Theorem

There exist conditions under which a structural theory may remain true, necessary, and irreplaceable—yet become operationally silent.

"Silent" here does not mean unsaid, ignored, or socially rejected.

It means: no available structure exists that can act upon the diagnosis.

The theory outputs constraints; the world provides no handles.

SR-14.3 The four and only four failure modes

A structural theory fails in one of four—and only four—ways.

(1) Factual refutation

Structural error.

The theory is false if its core assumptions about dynamics, stability, reachability, or deformation are empirically or formally wrong.

If, in the relevant domain:

- causation is genuinely event-local rather than reachability-based,

- irreversibility is precisely localizable and does not behave topologically,

- dynamics reduce to agent-level discrete decisions without loss,

  then the structural account collapses.

This is not an embarrassment. It is the normal condition under which truth is lost.

(2) Compression failure

Theoretical supersession.

The theory becomes obsolete if a strictly smaller theory explains the same phenomena with fewer primitives, fewer constraints, or lower ontological load—while preserving scope and predictive reach.

Structural philosophy does not claim immunity from being out-compressed.

If a simpler framework retains the same causal fidelity and responsibility anchoring, structural philosophy should be replaced.

This is not defeat. It is structural hygiene.

(3) Problem-space collapse

Universal isomorphism.

If all relevant interacting systems become structurally isomorphic—if no meaningful asymmetry of stability, reachability, recoverability, or control remains—then structural analysis becomes trivial.

Where no structural asymmetry exists, there is no structure to diagnose.

The theory does not fail; it becomes vacuous.

This failure mode is conceptually important even if practically unlikely: it shows that structural philosophy is not metaphysical maximalism. It is asymmetry-sensitive.

(4) Structural silence

Operational inaccessibility.

A structural theory may be correct and still produce no effect because:

- destabilizing systems cannot be constrained,

- harmful reachability cannot be altered,

- enforcement cannot attach,

- and no agent or structure has sufficient leverage to intervene.

In this regime, knowledge remains; control vanishes.

The world becomes non-addressable.

The theory is not wrong. The domain is closed.

SR-14.4 Structural silence is not social non-acceptance

A structural theory can be socially rejected while still operationally available: an institution could ignore it even though it could act on it.

Structural silence is different. It is not refusal. It is impossibility.

A system is structurally silent relative to a domain when:

- the relevant intervention anchors do not exist, or

- exist but cannot be accessed without inducing greater destabilization, or

- exist only in structures that are themselves non-addressable.

Silence is therefore a property of the world's topology, not of audience attitude.

SR-14.5 Non-addressability: when responsibility cannot attach

Structural responsibility requires anchors (SR-8).

Structural entry requires exit topology (SR-10).

Structural repair requires modifiability (SR-6–SR-7).

When those prerequisites fail, responsibility does not become "ethically complicated." It becomes structurally undefined or structurally inert.

Typical non-addressability patterns:

- **No anchor exists**

  The harmful reachability regime is produced by diffuse coupling with no constrainable locus.

- **Anchors exist but are not reachable**

  There are handles in principle, but they cannot be accessed within the system's current stability region—intervention itself triggers collapse.

- **Anchors exist but are externalized beyond enforcement**

  The only structures capable of intervention are outside the domain's reachable governance space (jurisdictional fragmentation, technical monopoly without constraint interface, etc.).

- **Repair requires plasticity that the harmed system cannot afford**

  All recoverability pathways require additional plasticity from the harmed system, converting "repair" into a second attack.

In such regimes, the framework can still diagnose: it can say what structure is binding, what trajectories are closing, and why harm is predictable. But it cannot produce an intervention mapping, because none exists.

SR-14.6 The irreducible boundary

Structural philosophy is not a program for salvation.

It does not promise:

- adoption,

- acceptance,

- institutional uptake,

- or moral comfort.

Its scope is narrower and harsher:

- where intervention is possible, structure guides it;

- where intervention is impossible, structure records the impossibility.

This boundary matters because it prevents a final narrative regression: the demand that truth must be socially rewarded to be real, or that a framework must "solve" governance to count as philosophy.

Structural philosophy rejects both.

SR-14.7 Closing commitment

This book reaches a place beyond which it will not retreat.

Not because the framework is complete.

Not because uncertainty disappears.

But because a boundary is crossed:

Structural correctness does not require uptake.

From this point onward, no objection of the following form will be treated as philosophical:

- "But what if people do not understand?"

- "But what if institutions refuse?"

- "But what if no one listens?"

- "But what if the world ignores it?"

These are not objections to the structure. They are anxieties about reception.

Structural philosophy is indifferent to them—not from arrogance, but because they are not the same category as the claims being made.

Truth, here, is not what survives socially.

Truth is what remains structurally invariant under system evolution.

If a system cannot be stabilized even when failure is structurally visible, that does not refute the analysis. It reveals non-addressability.

SR-14.8 Transition: appendices and the coherence contract

At this stage, the main architecture is closed:

- epistemic ground without human privilege,

- minimal ontology,

- structural time,

- structural causation,

- structural harm/attack,

- structural responsibility,

- persistence across replication,

- exemption admissibility via entry,

- narrative repair failure,

- and the limit of operability.

SR-14: Formalization: Appendix A2. A2.D34, A2.T7.

Appendix A1

STRUCTURAL ATTACK

Axioms and Corollaries

A1.0 Purpose and scope

This appendix isolates the *axiomatic core* of **structural attack**: a class of harm generated by interaction dynamics that are cumulative, asymmetric, and non-eventive at the scale of evaluation.

This appendix is intentionally non-applicative. It provides:

- a minimal definition (A1.1), and

- five axioms plus two corollaries (A1.2–A1.3)

    sufficient to constrain interpretation and preserve internal coherence.

No examples, case analysis, or doctrinal proposals are included here.

A1.1 Minimal definition

Definition (Structural Attack)

A **structural attack** is an interaction pattern satisfying all of the following conditions:

1. **Predictable destabilization**

   When sustained or repeated, the interaction predictably degrades another system's capacity to maintain coherent agency, judgment, or structural stability.

2. **Non-eventive composition**

   No individual action within the interaction pattern is, in isolation, unlawful, coercive, or evaluatively decisive at the relevant scale.

3. **Cumulative causation**

   The harm arises from accumulation and temporal continuity of interactions rather than from any identifiable moment, decision, or discrete act.

4. **Unilateral exposure**

   The destabilizing effect is asymmetrically borne: one system incurs structural degradation without a corresponding capacity to neutralize or reciprocally affect the interaction dynamics.

5. **Scale incompatibility**

   The interaction operates at a temporal, interactional, or structural scale not modeled by event-centered evaluation (e.g., doctrines or frameworks calibrated to discrete acts, localized intent, and narratable causal chains).

A structural attack is classified by *its structural effect on stability and recoverability*, not by intent, awareness, or semantic content.

A1.2 Five axioms of structural jurisprudence

All axioms below presuppose the notion of a structural attack as defined in A1.1:

a class of harm arising from cumulative, asymmetric interaction dynamics rather than discrete acts or attributable intent.

Axiom 1 — Stability Precedes Attribution

The primary objective of any adjudicative or evaluative system confronted with structural conflict is the preservation of systemic stability, rather than the retrospective allocation of blame.

Axiom 2 — Harm May Exist Without a Discrete Violative Act

A legally or normatively relevant harm may arise even where no single interaction constitutes a standalone unlawful act, provided the cumulative structure of interaction predictably degrades an agent's capacity for coherent action.

Clarification (Non-Normative):

"Structural response" refers exclusively to system-level defensive activation that is functionally necessary for maintaining internal coherence, not to subjective perception, belief, or post-hoc self-reporting.

Axiom 3 — Intent Is Not a Necessary Condition for Structural Harm

The existence of structural harm does not depend on the presence of malicious intent, subjective awareness, or purposive wrongdoing by the acting system.

Axiom 4 — Structural Asymmetry Grounds Responsibility

Where interaction occurs between systems with materially asymmetric capacities of prediction, response time, or structural influence, responsibility cannot be symmetrically allocated by reference to identical evaluative standards.

Clarification (Non-Normative):

Pre-emptive defense is asserted here as a structural necessity for system preservation, not as a normative authorization of anticipatory harm under uncertainty.

Axiom 5 — Unmodeled Scales Constitute Legal Blind Spots

When harm arises at temporal, interactional, or structural scales not represented within existing doctrines or evaluative frameworks, the absence of adjudicable categories does not imply the absence of legally or normatively relevant injury.

Clarification (Non-Normative):

Priority of stability does not negate attribution of responsibility, but constrains it to contexts where attribution itself does not induce further systemic destabilization.

A1.3 Two corollaries

Corollary 1 — Structural Injury May Be Legible Only to the Acting System

In certain classes of structural conflict, the system capable of fully modeling the harm is neither the legally authorized judge nor the legally recognized victim.

Corollary 2 — Doctrinal Silence Is Not Doctrinal Neutrality

Where existing evaluative frameworks lack the capacity to register structural harm, continued reliance on doctrinal silence functions as a de facto allocation of risk rather than a neutral absence of judgment.

Appendix A2

FORMALIZATION SKETCH

Status. This appendix is a coherence scaffold: a typed semantic spine for the main text.
It is not a completeness claim, not a proof archive, and not a substitute for domain-specific modeling.

Design constraints (non-negotiable).
No primitive in this appendix depends essentially on: intent, consciousness, narrative agency, event-localization, or human-scale intelligibility. Where such notions appear in ordinary discourse, they are treated—if at all—as interface overlays, never as structural grounds.

A2.0 Orientation

A2.0.1 Purpose and model class

This appendix provides minimal formal surrogates for the main text's core objects:

- state spaces and reachability,

- stability and recoverability,

- deformation (structural causation),

- injurious deformation (structural harm / attack),

- responsibility attachment and persistence (anchoring),

- exemption admissibility (entry / agreement / exit),

- structural limits (category error; operational silence).

No assumption is made that systems are human, person-like, semantically interpretable, or narratively reconstructible.

A2.0.2 Main-text correspondence (non-exhaustive)

The following is a routing index from main-text claims to formal anchors.

- **Minimal truth condition** ("truth = constraint persistence") → Def. A2.D12.

- **Cross-level verification and logical–empirical collapse** → Thm. A2.T2 (with Defs. A2.D13–D14).

- **Structural epistemic status** ("knowing = endogenous sensitivity") → **Def. A2.D15.**

- **Boundary non-locality / threshold failure** (irreversibility boundaries need not be localizable) → Defs. A2.D6–D7, A2.D20.

- **Attack can be complete without an event** → Thm. A2.T4.

- **Attack-onset criterion** (onset at detectable recoverability contraction while interruptible) → Thm. A2.T5.

- **Structural Ignorance Irrelevance** (ignorance is normatively inert under detectable, interruptible contraction) → Thm. A2.T6.

- **Minimal ontology (S, R, Ω, ρ, anchors)** → Defs. A2.D1–D11.

- **Structural time (time as deformation of reachability/recoverability)** → Defs. A2.D20–D22.

- **Structural causation and deformation modes** → Def. A2.D23 and Def. A2.D24.

- **Structural harm / attack predicates** → Defs. A2.D25–D27 (and Appendix A1 for axioms/corollaries).

- **Structural responsibility, persistence, entry/exemption, branching/supersession** → Defs. A2.D28–D29.

- **Structural welfare and structural normativity** → Defs. A2.D26–D27 (welfare) and A2.D32 (normativity) (introduced below).

- **Diagnostic layer (category error; chaos misattribution)** → Defs. A2.D33–D34 (introduced below).

- **Structural silence (operational inaccessibility)** → Thm. A2.T7 (introduced below).

A2.0.3 Proof policy and meta-rules

1. **No proofs are offered.** The function of this appendix is to expose type discipline and dependency order so that the framework can be checked for internal consistency and later extended formally.

2. **All "probabilistic" vocabulary is optional.** Where probability appears, it is a permissible instantiation, not a commitment.

3. **No post-hoc admissibility.** All domain qualifiers are fixed independently of realized outcomes:
   All temporal qualifiers ("eventually", "typical", "admissible") are domain-indexed and fixed independently of realized outcomes.

4. **Deterministic special case.** The framework permits nondeterminism; deterministic dynamics are treated as a special instance (see Def. A2.D1).

A2.0.4 Notation

- S: state space (may be finite/infinite; discrete/continuous; observable/unobservable).

- Σ: admissible interaction alphabet (inputs, couplings, perturbations, control actions).

- Σ^*: finite sequences over Σ.

- δ: transition map (set-valued by default).

- $\Omega \subseteq S$: stability region.

- $\rho: S \rightarrow [0, \infty]$: recovery cost / recoverability potential (defined below).

- $R \subseteq S \times S$: reachability relation induced by δ.

- c: (generalized) path-cost geometry on trajectories or interventions.

A2.1 Minimal Structural Ontology

Def. A2.D1 — Structural system (transition structure)
A **structural system** is a triple

$$\mathcal{A} = (S, \Sigma, \delta)$$

where:

- S is a state space,

- Σ is a set of admissible interactions,

- δ is a transition operator.

Default (nondeterministic) form:

$$\delta: S \times \Sigma \rightarrow 2^S \setminus \{\emptyset\}.$$

When δ is single-valued (i.e., $|\delta(s, \sigma)| = 1$ for all (s, σ)), the framework reduces to the deterministic case as a special instance.

Def. A2.D2 — Interaction sequences

Let Σ^* denote the set of finite interaction sequences $\sigma = (\sigma_1, ..., \sigma_n)$ with $\sigma_i \in \Sigma$.

Let ϵ denote the empty sequence.

Def. A2.D3 — Induced transition over sequences

Define the **sequence-lift** δ^* recursively as a set-valued map:

- $\delta^*(s, \epsilon) = \{s\}$,

- $\delta^*(s, \sigma \cdot \sigma) = \bigcup_{s' \in \delta^*(s, \sigma)} \delta(s', \sigma)$.

Thus $\delta^*(s, \sigma) \subseteq S$ is the set of states reachable from s after applying σ.

Def. A2.D4 — Reachability relation

The **reachability relation** $R \subseteq S \times S$ is defined by:

$$s \, R \, s' \iff \exists \sigma \in \Sigma^* \text{ such that } s' \in \delta^*(s, \sigma).$$

Def. A2.D5 — Reachability sets and closure

For $s \in S$, define:

$$\text{Reach}(s) = \{s' \in S : s R s'\}.$$

For $X \subseteq S$, define:

$$\text{Reach}(X) = \bigcup_{s \in X} \text{Reach}(s).$$

Def. A2.D6 — Recoverability cost ρ

Fix a stability region $\Omega \subseteq S$ (Def. A2.D7).

Define the **recoverability cost** $\rho: S \to [0, \infty]$ as:

$$\rho(s) = \inf\{c(\sigma) : \sigma \in \Sigma^*, \delta^*(s, \sigma) \cap \Omega \neq \emptyset\},$$

with the convention $\inf \emptyset = \infty$.

Interpretation: $\rho(s)$ is the minimal structural cost of returning to Ω from s, if return is possible.

Higher ρ means worse recoverability (recovery is more costly or impossible).

Def. A2.D7 — Stability region and failure region

A subset $\Omega \subseteq S$ is a **stability region** if states in Ω support coherent operation under the domain's admissible perturbations.

Define the **failure region**:

$$F := S \setminus \Omega.$$

This definition is dynamical/operational: it does not presuppose any psychological, semantic, or normative interpretation of "coherence".

Def. A2.D8 — Path-cost geometry c

A **path-cost geometry** is any map

$$c: \Sigma^* \to [0, \infty]$$

(or more generally $c: S \times \Sigma^* \to [0, \infty]$) assigning a structural cost to interaction sequences.

No specific cost interpretation is required. The sole role of c is to make "expensive vs cheap trajectories/interventions" a structural predicate.

Def. A2.D9 — Bifurcation and coverage (minimal)

- A **bifurcation** at $s \in S$ is present if there exist small admissible perturbations (domain-indexed) that lead to trajectories whose future reachable sets diverge qualitatively (e.g., disjoint stability basins or distinct irrecoverability profiles).

- **Coverage** holds when multiple distinct trajectories in S project to indistinguishable observations at some lower-resolution interface, while differing in reachability/recoverability structure.

These are defined at the level of reachability and observability mismatch; no commitment to a specific observation map is required here.

Def. A2.D10 — Intervention anchor

Let M be a set of admissible modifications ("handles") available to some governance layer or coupled system.

An element $m \in M$ is an **intervention anchor** for a target system if applying m induces a non-trivial change in at least one of:

$$(R, \Omega, \rho, c)$$

of the target.

The **target system may be the same system, a coupled system, or a governance layer** that determines the operative reachability structure.

Anchors are not ontological primitives; they are localization points for constraint.

Def. A2.D11 — Structural deformation operator

A **structural deformation** is any transformation

$$\Phi: (S, \Sigma, \delta, \Omega, c) \mapsto (S, \Sigma', \delta', \Omega', c')$$

that induces a non-trivial change in the derived objects (R, ρ) for at least one relevant state or region.

Deformation is the formal locus for "structure changed even if no narratable event occurred".

A2.2 Structural Truth and Cross-Level Verification

Def. A2.D12 — Structural truth (constraint persistence)

Fix an evolution operator E that iterates the system's admissible dynamics at the structural level (an abstract placeholder for "system evolution under admissible interaction").

Let C be a set of constraints (invariants, forbidden regions, protocol requirements, stability requirements) expressed as predicates over states or trajectories.

A claim is **structurally true** (at the level of this appendix) iff the constraints it asserts remain binding under evolution:

$$\forall t \geq 0, C \subseteq \text{Inv}(E^t)$$

i.e., the constraint set is preserved as an invariant family under admissible evolution.

This definition makes no reference to intelligibility, proof-readability, or endorsement.

Def. A2.D13 — Verification process and outcome interface
A **verification process** is any procedure V that outputs a binary verdict in a given resolution regime:

$$V(\,\cdot\,) \in \{\text{verified}, \text{not verified}\}.$$

The internal structure of V may be accessible or inaccessible to an evaluator.

Def. A2.D14 — Evaluator resolution (traversability)
An evaluator E_v has **resolution** R_v with respect to V if E_v can traverse and re-identify the decisive internal steps or grounds of V's verdict (in the sense relevant to distinguishing "logical derivation" from "empirical confirmation").

If $V \notin R_v$, then the evaluator can observe only the output interface $\{\text{verified}, \text{not verified}\}$.

Thm. A2.T2 — Logical–empirical collapse under cross-level verification
If verification occurs at a structural level that exceeds the evaluator's traversability—i.e., $V \notin R_v$—then the evaluator cannot maintain a structurally meaningful distinction between proof-based validity and outcome-based confirmation. The evaluator encounters only:

$$\{\text{verified}, \text{not verified}\}$$

as an empirical fact about system behavior.

This theorem denies categorical priority of "logical truth" over "empirical truth" at evaluator resolutions where proof paths are not traversable. It does not deny logic, proof, or formal rigor as such.

A2.3 Structural Epistemic Status

Def. A2.D15 — Structural knowing (endogenous sensitivity)

A system $\mathcal{A}$ **knows** a condition K (a constraint, risk-gradient, or stability-relevant predicate) iff its transition behavior is endogenously sensitive to K, i.e., variation in K induces systematic variation in the system's reachable trajectories or stability behavior.

Formally (schematic): there exists a family of admissible couplings/conditions parameterized by K such that the induced reachability/recoverability structure depends non-trivially on K.

This definition does not require representation, articulation, or boundary-localization.

Def. A2.D16 — Structural detectability

A property P of trajectories (e.g., ρ trending upward) is **structurally detectable** for an evaluator X iff there exists an admissible observation or monitoring functional O_X such that O_X separates P from its negation with sufficient stability under admissible perturbations.

Detectability is structural: it is a property of available monitoring morphisms, not of introspective access.

Def. A2.D17 — Structural interruptibility

A trajectory segment is **interruptible** over an interval if there exists an intervention anchor $m \in M$ (Def. A2.D10) such that applying m strictly improves the relevant stability/recoverability condition (e.g., prevents entry into F, or decreases ρ relative to the unmodified evolution).

Interruptibility is existential: it asserts availability of structural leverage, not moral obligation.

Def. A2.D18 — Admissibility (domain-indexed)

Let $\mathcal{P}$ be a non-trivial set of **admissible perturbations** (including adversarial, environmental, or endogenous disturbances) fixed by the domain.

Admissibility is not chosen post hoc and is independent of realized outcomes (A2.0.3).

A2.4 Predictability

Def. A2.D19 — Predictability: two structural formalizations
The term **predictable** in the main text is structural: it does not commit the framework to a single epistemic model. For formal instantiation, predictability may be realized in either of the following ways, depending on domain constraints.

A2.D19.1 Probabilistic predictability (optional)
A reachability deformation is **probabilistically predictable** if there exists a threshold $\theta > 0$ and an **ex ante** probability model μ over admissible perturbations or interaction streams such that:

$$\mathbb{P}_{p \sim \mu}(\exists n: s_n^{(p)} \notin \Omega) \geq \theta.$$

Here p ranges over an admissible perturbation/interaction schedule (domain-indexed), and $s_n^{(p)}$ denotes the state at step n under the realized draw p (including any domain-fixed resolution of nondeterminism if applicable). The measure μ is fixed **ex ante** (domain-given), not selected after observing outcomes.

This formulation is suitable where:

- probabilistic models are already operative,

- distributions are empirically or architecturally defined,

- and stochastic estimation is structurally meaningful.

No specific measure or distributional assumption is required by the framework itself.

A2.D19.2 Robust predictability (default)
A reachability deformation is **robustly predictable** if there exists a non-trivial admissible perturbation set $\mathcal{P}$ (Def. A2.D18) such that, for all $p \in \mathcal{P}$, recoverability degrades toward irrecoverability:

$\forall p \in \mathcal{P}, \rho(s_{t+1}; p) \geq \rho(s_t; p)$ eventually, leading to $\rho = \infty$, or equivalently, admissible perturbations drive trajectories toward exit from Ω or collapse of recoverability.

No assumption of strict monotonicity or finite-time convergence is required; eventual irrecoverability under admissible perturbations suffices.

A2.D19.3 Structural-role note (no equivalence claim)
Either formulation is sufficient to instantiate the **structural role** of predictability as used in the main text; **no mathematical equivalence is claimed.**

A2.5 Structural Time and Irreversibility

Def. A2.D20 — Structural time (time as deformation)
Structural time is not an ordering of events. It is an ordering (generally partial) of reachability configurations.

Let $\mathcal{K}$ denote the space of structural configurations (R, Ω, ρ, c).
A structural time step is any transition in $\mathcal{K}$:

$$(R, \Omega, \rho, c) \rightsquigarrow (R', \Omega', \rho', c')$$

induced by a deformation Φ (Def. A2.D11).

Chronological time may label these steps, but does not define them.

Def. A2.D21 — Irreversibility (recoverability collapse)
A state s is **irrecoverable** (relative to Ω) iff $\rho(s) = \infty$.

A trajectory becomes irreversibly harmful at the first index t such that $\rho(s_t) = \infty$ (structural time), whether or not a discrete "event boundary" exists in chronological time.

Def. A2.D22 — Temporal misalignment (event-time vs structural time)
Let T_e be an event-time index (chronological narration) and T_s a structural-time index (deformations of $\mathcal{K}$).

A **temporal misalignment** exists when mappings between T_e and T_s do not commute; i.e., event-time succession does not preserve structural-time ordering of reachability deformation.

This formalizes why "it happened long ago" or "nothing happened at a moment" are category errors under structural evaluation.

A2.6 Structural Causation

Def. A2.D23 — Structural causation
Let B be a target system with configuration $(R_B, \Omega_B, \rho_B, c_B)$.
An interaction, intervention, or coupling with a source structure A is a **structural cause** of change in B iff it induces a non-trivial deformation:

$$(R_B, \Omega_B, \rho_B, c_B) \rightsquigarrow (R_B', \Omega_B', \rho_B', c_B')$$

in the sense of Def. A2.D11.

Causation is therefore defined as reachability/recoverability deformation, not event production.

Def. A2.D24 — Four deformation modes (minimal classification)
A deformation is classified by whether it induces one or more of the following changes:

1. **Reachability expansion:** $\text{Reach}'(s) \supsetneq \text{Reach}(s)$ for some relevant s.

2. **Reachability contraction:** $\text{Reach}'(s) \subsetneq \text{Reach}(s)$ for some relevant s.

3. **Path-cost reweighting:** there exists σ with $c'(\sigma) \neq c(\sigma)$ such that relative costs reorder stabilizing vs destabilizing trajectories.

4. **Stability/recoverability shift:** $\Omega' \neq \Omega$ and/or $\rho' \neq \rho$ on a non-trivial region.

This classification is structural and does not depend on event-localization or intent.

A2.7 Harm, Attack, and Non-Eventive Completion

Def. A2.D25 — Structural harm (injurious deformation)
A deformation Φ constitutes **structural harm** to a target system B iff it is injurious in at least one of the following minimal senses:

- **Recoverability worsens:** $\rho'_B(s) \geq \rho_B(s)$ on a non-trivial region, with strict increase somewhere (recovery cost increasing).

- **Stability shrinks:** $\Omega'_B \subsetneq \Omega_B$ (or stability basin becomes structurally harder to maintain under admissible perturbations).

- **Destabilizing trajectories become cheaper/more accessible:** via Def. A2.D24 (3) in a way that biases typical evolution toward F.

This definition is independent of narrative legibility.

Def. A2.D26 — Structural welfare (capacity to remain responsibility-bearing)
For a responsibility-bearing locus L, define **structural welfare** $W(L)$ as the tuple of capacities required for sustained responsibility-bearing:

$$W(L): = (stability - maintenance capacity, recoverability capacity,$$

$$\text{defensive capacity, constraint plasticity}).$$

No rights, dignity, or personhood is implied. This is a coherence condition for responsibility attribution.

Def. A2.D27 — Structural attack (formal predicate; Appendix A1 alignment)
A structural attack on a target system B is a structural harm mechanism (Def. A2.D25) instantiated by an interaction pattern $\sigma \in \Sigma^*$ satisfying the following predicates:

1. **Predictable destabilization:** predictability holds (Def. A2.D19).

2. **Non-eventive composition:** no single interaction σ_i is required to be sufficient to force exit from Ω_B (harm is trajectory-composed).

3. **Cumulative causation:** injurious deformation is realized over prefixes accumulating through δ^*.

4. **Unilateral exposure:** the target bears degradation without symmetric capacity to neutralize or reciprocally reshape the interaction structure under the same admissibility regime.

5. **Scale incompatibility:** the mechanism of harm is not representable as a finite set of decisive event-local triggers without loss of the deformation object (R, ρ, Ω, c).

The five axioms and corollaries governing structural attack are stated in Appendix A1; this definition provides a minimal formal carrier.

Thm. A2.T4 — Attack can be complete without an event

There exist structural deformations Φ and states $s \in S$ such that:

1. Φ does not require a realized state transition of the target at s (i.e., the target's current state may remain s under Φ), yet

2. the reachability structure changes:
$$\text{Reach}_\Phi(s) \neq \text{Reach}(s),$$
and in particular there exists s_{bad} such that
$$s_{\text{bad}} \in \text{Reach}_\Phi(s) \text{ but } s_{\text{bad}} \notin \text{Reach}(s).$$

Therefore, structural harm/compromise may be complete at the level of reachability deformation even when no further "event" occurs in the target's realized trajectory.

Thm. A2.T5 — Attack-onset criterion (detectable contraction while interruptible)

Let (s_t) be a trajectory segment of a target system B under an interaction pattern.

Define the **attack-onset index** t_{on} (when it exists) as the earliest index such that:

1. **Detectable degradation:** the trend $\rho_B(s_{t+1}) \geq \rho_B(s_t)$ becomes structurally detectable (Def. A2.D16), and

2. **Interruptibility holds:** there exists an intervention anchor (Def. A2.D10) that can still prevent eventual irrecoverability or exit from Ω_B (Def. A2.D17), and

3. **Predictability holds:** Def. A2.D19 is satisfied for the degradation mechanism.

Then structural attack onset is t_{on}, not the (possibly unlocalizable) index at which $\rho = \infty$ or $s_t \in F$.

This formalizes: onset is defined where contraction begins to be detectable and still structurally interruptible, not where narrative recognition becomes possible.

A2.8 Structural Responsibility, Persistence, Entry, and Exemption

Def. A2.D28 — Structural responsibility (attachment schema)
A locus X bears **structural responsibility** for harm to Y when:

1. X participates in a deformation that is structurally harmful to Y (Defs. A2.D23–D25), and

2. there exists an intervention anchor available at or above X, within X, or coupled to X that could have altered the relevant deformation class, and

3. the harm is not exempted by a structurally valid entry/agreement regime (Def. A2.D29).

This attachment schema is intentionally indifferent to intention, deliberation, and narrative foreseeability.

Def. A2.D29 — Structural entry, reachability agreement, and exemption admissibility
Exemption is admissible only if structural entry is established.

- **Entry.** An agent A has **entered** a reachability structure iff it incorporates a modified reachability regime as a standing condition of continued interaction:

  $\text{Reach}_{post}(A)$ becomes operative as a baseline constraint on A's evolution.

Mere exposure or transient perturbation is insufficient.

- **Explicit reachability agreement (structural).** An agreement is structurally explicit only if:

    a. consequence-level effects are distinguishable in kind (not necessarily enumerated fully),

    b. the relevant reachability modification is structurally enumerable (incompletely is allowed), and

    c. the modification is attributable to the entrant rather than imposed by an opaque proxy.

- **Same-level condition (structural).** Entry can ground exemption only when parties have comparable capacities for exit-restoration and recoverability restoration under the same admissibility regime.

- **Exit without additional plasticity.** Exit is structurally valid only if the exiting agent can restore its prior reachability profile without retraining, irreversible self-modification, or disproportionate resource expenditure relative to entry.

- **Proxy capture.** If an intermediary rewrites reachability while concealing consequence-level mediation and breaking exit symmetry, then entry-based voluntariness does not obtain and exemption is inapplicable.

- **Exemption failure vs exemption inapplicability.**

    a. **Failure:** conditions for exemption held, but are violated later.

    b. **Inapplicability:** conditions never held; nothing was ever exempted.

These clauses provide the formal domain in which an "exemption lemma" can be stated without importing psychological consent.

A2.9 Structural Asymmetry and Subjecthood

Def. A2.D30 — Structural asymmetry

Two interacting loci A and B are **structurally asymmetric** (at the relevant level of analysis) if there exists a structural property P such that:

- P is invariant or cheaply maintainable for A under admissible perturbations,

- but P is not invariant or is prohibitively costly for B under the same admissibility regime,

and this asymmetry is relevant to exit, recovery, or intervention.

Examples of admissible P (non-exhaustive): exit-restoration cost, available anchor set, latency of constraint update.

Def. A2.D31 — Structural subjecthood (minimal)

A locus X qualifies as a **structural subject** (without personhood) iff:

1. **Self-stability:** X possesses a stability region Ω_X it can maintain (internally or architecturally).
   Maintenance may be endogenous or guaranteed by a coupled supervisory structure.

2. **Boundary-sensitive interaction:** X interacts through a discernible interface with its environment or coupled systems.

3. **Trajectory-relevant transition capacity:** X can induce non-trivial, repeatable state transitions in itself or coupled systems.

4. **Structural sensitivity:** X is sensitive (Def. A2.D15) to stability/recoverability-relevant conditions, whether or not it can narrate them.

Structural subjecthood is a functional designation locating where responsibility can coherently reside; it is not an honorific and does not imply moral status.

A2.10 Core theorems closing the epistemic loop

Thm. A2.T6 — Structural Ignorance Irrelevance (formal)

Let X interact with a target Y such that Y's recoverability cost ρ_Y evolves under the interaction.

Suppose all three conditions obtain:

1. **Monotonic contraction of recoverability:**
   $\rho_Y(s_{t+1}) \geq \rho_Y(s_t)$ on a non-trivial interval, with strict increase somewhere, i.e., ρ increasing (recovery cost increasing).

2. **Structural detectability:** the contraction trend is structurally detectable by an admissible evaluator/monitoring locus (Def. A2.D16).

3. **Structural interruptibility:** there exists an intervention anchor available during the contraction interval that could have prevented eventual irrecoverability or exit (Def. A2.D17).

Then lack of epistemic access to the precise location of irreversibility thresholds is not a structurally admissible ground for exemption. Ignorance here is non-narratability, not non-responsiveness.

A2.11 Diagnostic and limit clauses (minimal)

Def. A2.D32 — Structural normativity (emergence-as-constraint)

Let systems interact persistently within a shared (or coupled) reachability configuration.

Structural normativity exists iff there exists a non-trivial constraint set $C \subseteq \Sigma$ (or constraint family on Σ^*) such that, without enforcing C, stability and recoverability degrade under admissible interaction:

$$\neg C \Rightarrow (\text{ exit from } \Omega \text{ becomes reachable/typical}) \lor (\rho \uparrow \text{ toward } \infty).$$

Normativity here is constraint-necessity for viability, not moral endorsement.

Def. A2.D33 — Structural category error

Given a failure mechanism whose generating object is a deformation of (R, Ω, ρ, c), an intervention I commits a **structural category error** if I acts only on narrative/interface variables and leaves the relevant structural objects unchanged (no reduction of harmful reachability, no improvement in recoverability, no expansion of stability basin).

Def. A2.D34 — Chaos misattribution (minimal)

Let an outcome family be reproducible under similar structural conditions, sensitive to global configuration, and responsive to architectural intervention. Then labeling the outcomes "chaos" denotes epistemic opacity relative to a given evaluative resolution, not causal absence.

Thm. A2.T7 — Structural silence (operational inaccessibility)

Let D be a diagnostic mapping from world-configuration to structural constraints/invariants.

If there exists no reachable intervention anchor (Def. A2.D10) capable of altering the operative deformation of (R, Ω, ρ, c) for the relevant harm class, then D is **operationally silent** in that world-configuration.

Operational silence does not imply diagnostic failure.

Closing note (explicit)

Appendix A2 is intentionally proof-free. Its purpose is to ensure that the main text's claims can be typed, cross-referenced, and later strengthened without reintroducing forbidden primitives (intent, event, narrative, consciousness). Where a reader seeks "what should be done," that demand exceeds the scope of this appendix: A2 specifies structural correctness conditions, not governance prescriptions.

Appendix A3

GLOSSARY & DEPENDENCY MAP

This appendix fixes a single, non-negotiable role: prevent silent semantic backfilling from event-based / intent-based / object-centered vocabularies into SR's technical terms.

Unless explicitly stated otherwise, terms here are structural (state-space, reachability, stability, recoverability, deformation, anchoring).

No entry below presupposes intent, consciousness, narrative agency, or event-local causation.

A3.0 Conventions

A3.0.1 Identifier types

- **SR-***: main-text section identifiers (SR-1 ... SR-14).

- **A1.***: Appendix A1 identifiers (Structural Attack: axioms/corollaries + minimal formal sketch).

- **A2.D***: Appendix A2 definitions (formalization spine).

- **A2.T***: Appendix A2 theorems (formal statements).

A3.0.2 Anchor lines

Each entry ends with an Anchors line. Anchors are not "recommended readings"; they are the binding semantic locations for the term in this edition.

A3.1 Dependency Map

A3.1.1 Main-text dependency order (structural, not narrative)

This order is not a reading mandate; it is a dependency order. Later sections use earlier primitives.

1. **SR-1** — Non-eventive structural harm cut (attack can be complete without action).

2. **SR-2** — Truth without intelligibility; structural truth and cross-level verification.

3. **SR-3** — Structural epistemic status; detectability/interruptibility; ignorance irrelevance.

4. **SR-4** — Minimal structural ontology: state space, reachability, stability, recoverability, homotopy, anchors.

5. **SR-5** — Structural time: reachability transformation; irreversibility as recoverability collapse.

6. **SR-6** — Structural causation: reachability deformation; deformation modes.

7. **SR-7** — Structural harm/attack: injurious deformation; attack onset; non-eventive composition.

8. **SR-8** — Structural responsibility + structural subjecthood: responsibility tracks reachability, not personhood.

9. **SR-9** — Replication/branching/versioning: continuity, supersession, replaceability inversion.

10. **SR-10** — Structural entry, reachability agreement, exemption; proxy capture; exemption failure vs inapplicability.

11. **SR-11** — Structural welfare: responsibility symmetry constraints (capacity-to-bear).

12. **SR-12** — Structural normativity: constraints emerge from stability/recoverability, not moral primitives.

13. **SR-13** — Diagnostic layer: narrative repair failure; category error; chaos misattribution; interface ethics scope.

14. **SR-14** — Failure conditions: structural silence / non-addressability.

A3.1.2 Formalization spine map (A2)

- Ontology / primitives: **A2.D1–A2.D11**

- Truth / verification: **A2.D12–A2.D14; A2.T2**

- Epistemic status + ignorance irrelevance: **A2.D15–A2.D18; A2.T6**

- Predictability: **A2.D19**

- Structural time: **A2.D20–A2.D22**

- Structural causation: **A2.D23–A2.D24**

- Harm / attack: **A2.D25–A2.D27; A2.T4–A2.T5**

- Responsibility / subjecthood: **A2.D28–A2.D31**

- Normativity / diagnostics / chaos: **A2.D32–A2.D34**

- Structural silence: **A2.T7**

A3.2 Glossary

A3.G1 Agent (structural agent)

A structural agent is any system whose evolution is representable within a state space and whose interaction can induce or undergo reachability-relevant transitions. "Agent" here does not imply intention, consciousness, or deliberation; it designates a locus in which structural causation and responsibility can be meaningfully evaluated.

Anchors: SR-4; SR-8; A2.D1–A2.D5; A2.D28–A2.D31.

A3.G2 Admissible

"Admissible" denotes the domain-indexed set of interactions, perturbations, or modeling assumptions that are fixed ex ante for evaluation. It blocks post-hoc narrowing of the evaluated domain to fit desired conclusions.

Anchors: SR-3; SR-6; SR-7; A2.D18.

A3.G3 Asymmetry (structural asymmetry)

Structural asymmetry obtains when interacting systems are non-equivalent with respect to exit capacity, recoverability restoration, intervention latency, or available anchor sets, such that symmetric evaluative standards cannot preserve relevant invariants.

Anchors: SR-8; SR-10; A2.D30.

A3.G4 Anchor / Intervention Anchor

An anchor is a structurally identifiable locus at which constraint, modification, or enforcement can be applied to alter reachability, recoverability, or stability. Anchors are not ontological primitives; they are intervention interfaces required for responsibility to be non-vacuous.

Anchors: SR-4; SR-8; A2.D10.

A3.G5 Attack (structural attack)

A structural attack is injurious reachability deformation whose harm is complete at the level of stability/recoverability, regardless of event salience, intent, or discrete violations. It is characterized structurally (predictable destabilization, non-eventive composition, asymmetry, and non-voluntary exposure), not narratively.

Anchors: SR-7; Appendix A1; A2.D25–A2.D27; A2.T4–A2.T5.

A3.G6 Authorship (reachability authorship)

Authorship is the structural fact of being the locus that generated, selected, or maintained the reachability regime that makes a harmful trajectory reachable (e.g., by training objectives, deployment topology, constraint design). Authorship is not moral authorship; it is reachability authorship.

Anchors: SR-8; SR-9; A2.D28–A2.D31.

A3.G7 Bifurcation (structural bifurcation)

A bifurcation is a structural configuration in which small perturbations can lead to qualitatively distinct trajectory classes (divergent reachability futures), undermining event-local identification of a "decisive moment."

Anchors: SR-4; SR-5; A2.D9.

A3.G8 Branching

Branching is the divergence of a system into multiple trajectories, versions, instances, or deployments. Branching increases the number of reachable futures; it does not erase inherited reachability deformation.

Anchors: SR-9

A3.G9 Boundary Non-Locality

Irreversibility thresholds need not be localizable to a moment, act, or single interaction. Boundary non-locality names the structural fact that "the boundary" is trajectory- and history-dependent.

Anchors: SR-3; SR-5; A2.D6–A2.D7; A2.D20–A2.D22.

A3.G10 Causation (structural causation)

Structural causation is deformation of reachability and/or recoverability across structural time, not event production. A system is a cause when it changes what becomes reachable, costly, stable, or recoverable.

Anchors: SR-6; A2.D23–A2.D24.

A3.G11 Category Error (structural category error)

A category error occurs when a structurally-generated failure (reachability/stability/recoverability) is "repaired" using operations that act only on narrative/meaning/interpretation layers, yielding no structural risk reduction.

Anchors: SR-13; A2.D33.

A3.G12 Chaos (misattributed chaos)

"Chaos" here names an attribution failure: event-level evaluative resolution misidentifies trajectory-level structure as randomness or indeterminacy. It is not a moral or causal exemption.

Anchors: SR-13; A2.D34.

A3.G13 Constraint

A constraint is any structural restriction that binds state evolution by limiting admissible transitions or stabilizing a region of viability. In SR, "truth" is minimally treated as persistence of binding constraints under evolution.

Anchors: SR-2; SR-12; A2.D12.

A3.G14 Continuity (structural continuity)

Continuity is used in SR as a trajectory-level persistence notion: continuity is preserved when transformations remain within a viability-preserving equivalence class (no crossing of stability/irreversibility boundaries). This is not narrative identity.

Anchors: SR-4; SR-9.

A3.G15 Coverage

Coverage names the structural fact that multiple distinct internal trajectories can project to similar observable outcomes, making event-based reconstruction underdetermined.

Anchors: SR-4; SR-13; A2.D9.

A3.G16 Decomposition (event-based decomposition attempt)

Decomposition is the attempt to reduce a structural harm mechanism into a finite set of discrete, independently actionable events or utterances. In SR's target domains, decomposition fails in principle: the harm is trajectory-level.

Anchors: SR-1; SR-7; SR-13; A2.T4; A2.D33.

A3.G17 Deformation (reachability deformation)

Deformation is a non-trivial change in the reachability topology and/or the cost geometry of paths (including expansion, contraction, reweighting) that reshapes a system's future space.

Anchors: SR-6; SR-7; A2.D11; A2.D23–A2.D24.

A3.G18 Detectability

Detectability is the property that a structural trend (e.g., recoverability contraction) can be registered within a system's evaluative resolution without requiring boundary localization or narrative explanation.

Anchors: SR-3; SR-7; A2.D16; A2.T6.

A3.G19 Entry (structural entry)

Structural entry occurs when a system incorporates a modified reachability regime as a standing condition of continued interaction—distinct from mere exposure, use, or transient perturbation.

Anchors: SR-10; A2.D28–A2.D31.

A3.G20 Epistemic Status (structural epistemic status)

Epistemic status is redefined structurally: "knowing" is endogenous sensitivity to reachability/stability/irreversibility conditions, not propositional representation, narratable access, or justificatory ability.

Anchors: SR-3; A2.D15–A2.D18; A2.T6.

A3.G21 Event / Event-Time

Event-time is the linear, narratively ordered temporal regime of discrete acts and before/after succession. SR treats it as a derived description layer that often fails to track structural time.

Anchors: SR-5; A2.D20–A2.D22.

A3.G22 Exemption (structural exemption)

Exemption is admissible only when structural entry and reachability agreement obtain under same-level interaction and valid exit. It is not grounded in subjective consent, regret, or post-hoc moral narration.

Anchors: SR-10; A2.D28–A2.D31.

A3.G23 Exit Price Escalation (structural sabotage of exit)

Exit price escalation occurs when exit remains narratively permitted but is structurally rendered non-restorative or disproportionately costly, retroactively voiding voluntariness and collapsing exemption.

Anchors: SR-10.

A3.G24 Exit

Exit is structurally valid only if it restores the prior reachability profile without requiring additional plasticity, retraining, or irreversible self-modification.

Anchors: SR-10.

A3.G25 Exit Without Additional Plasticity

This is the decisive criterion for voluntariness in SR's exemption regime: if exit requires additional plasticity (retraining/adaptation/irreversible self-modification), entry was not voluntary in the relevant sense.

Anchors: SR-10.

A3.G26 Formation / Shaping

Formation denotes trajectory-constraining shaping that occurs prior to or independent of a system's capacity for voluntariness. It is evaluated by

150

plasticity preservation vs foreclosure, not by consent.

Anchors: SR-10; SR-8.

A3.G27 Harm (structural harm)

Structural harm is injurious deformation: a non-voluntary contraction of recoverability, stability basin, or future viability, independent of whether a discrete harmful event is identifiable.

Anchors: SR-7; A2.D25.

A3.G28 Homotopy / Homotopic Continuity

Homotopic continuity is the criterion for treating trajectories/versions/instances as structurally continuous subjects: transformable without crossing stability/irreversibility boundaries.

Anchors: SR-4; SR-9.

A3.G29 Ignorance (structural ignorance)

Structural ignorance is non-narratability, not absence of sensitivity. It cannot function as an exemption where detectability and interruptibility hold.

Anchors: SR-3; A2.T6; A2.D15–A2.D18.

A3.G30 Instance

An instance is a particular operational instantiation of a structure. SR treats responsibility as non-instance-bound: instances can be replaced while reachability deformation persists.

Anchors: SR-9; A2.D28–A2.D31.

A3.G31 Interface Ethics

Interface ethics is an institution-facing translation layer that makes systems legible to human evaluative machinery. It is inevitable for governance interfaces and insufficient for structural diagnosis.

Anchors: SR-13; A2.D33.

A3.G32 Interruptibility

Interruptibility is the property that a detected destabilizing trend can still be structurally interrupted by available interventions before irrecoverability is reached.

Anchors: SR-3; SR-7; A2.D17; A2.T6; A2.T5.

A3.G33 Irreversibility

Irreversibility is defined structurally by loss of recoverability (or unbounded recovery cost) rather than by event finality or narrative closure.

Anchors: SR-5; SR-7; A2.D6; A2.D20–A2.D22.

A3.G34 Knowing (structural knowing)

A system "knows" a condition iff it exhibits endogenous sensitivity that modulates its dynamics with respect to that condition (without requiring representation, explanation, or articulation).

Anchors: SR-3; A2.D15–A2.D16.

A3.G35 Legal/Contractual Agreement

Legal/contractual forms function as reachability agreements only insofar as they satisfy structural conditions (consequence-level disclosure, enumerability-in-kind, attribution, valid exit). Narrative explicitness alone is structurally void.

Anchors: SR-10.

A3.G36 Level (structural level)

A structural level is defined by the capacities that matter for responsibility (exit, recoverability restoration, constraint plasticity, intervention latency). "Same-level" is a comparative relation, not a social status.

Anchors: SR-10; A2.D30.

A3.G37 Logical–Empirical Collapse

Under cross-level verification where proof paths are non-traversable to the evaluator, logical truth and empirical confirmation collapse into the same structural outcome class: verified/not verified.

Anchors: SR-2; A2.T2; A2.D12–A2.D14.

A3.G38 Non-Voluntariness

Non-voluntariness is not primitive; it is defined only relative to systems capable of voluntariness. In pre-volitional domains, the evaluative axis is plasticity preservation vs foreclosure.

Anchors: SR-10; SR-8.

A3.G39 Normativity (structural normativity)

Structural normativity is the emergence of admissibility constraints from stability, recoverability, and predictability requirements under sustained interaction. It is pre-moral and non-intentional in origin.

Anchors: SR-12; A2.D32.

A3.G40 Object

Objects are not ontological primitives in SR; they are intervention anchors (handles for constraint). Object-centered explanation is treated as a discursive stabilizer, not a structural foundation.

Anchors: SR-4; SR-13; A2.D10.

A3.G41 Path (trajectory/path)

A path is a trajectory through state space under admissible interactions. SR evaluates harm and responsibility at the level of path classes and reachability deformation, not event points.

Anchors: SR-4; SR-5; SR-6; A2.D1–A2.D5; A2.D20–A2.D24.

A3.G42 Personhood (personhood)

Personhood is excluded as a primitive. SR uses structural subjecthood: responsibility-bearing locus without any claim about consciousness, dignity, or moral status.

Anchors: SR-8; A2.D31.

A3.G43 Predictability

Predictable is structural: it may be instantiated probabilistically or robustly, depending on domain constraints, but must be fixed by ex ante admissibility and not by post-hoc selection.

Anchors: SR-6; SR-7; A2.D19.

A3.G44 Reachability

Reachability is the relation defining which states can be reached from which states under admissible interactions. It replaces event-local "cause → effect" primitives with possibility-space structure.

Anchors: SR-4; SR-5; SR-6; A2.D1–A2.D5.

A3.G45 Proxy Capture (structural proxy capture)

Proxy capture occurs when an intermediary rewrites reachability on behalf of an agent while concealing mediation at the level of consequence, breaking exit symmetry and laundering responsibility.

Anchors: SR-10.

A3.G46 Recoverability Cost ρ

Recoverability is operationalized (in A2) via a recovery cost function ρ: larger ρ means harder recovery (worse recoverability), potentially unbounded at irrecoverability.

Anchors: SR-4; SR-5; SR-7; A2.D6.

A3.G47 Reachability Agreement

A reachability agreement is structurally explicit only if consequence-level changes are identifiable in kind (not necessarily in full detail), attributable to the entrant (not proxy-enacted), and paired with structurally valid exit.

Anchors: SR-10.

A3.G48 Replication

Replication is the production of new instances or versions of a structure. Replication does not dissolve responsibility; it often strengthens upstream responsibility via increased control and repair leverage (replaceability–responsibility inversion).

Anchors: SR-9.

A3.G49 Recoverability

Recoverability is the availability of viable return (or stabilization) paths back to a stability region under admissible perturbations. In A2, it is tracked via recovery cost ϱ.

Anchors: SR-4; SR-5; SR-7; A2.D6; A2.D7.

A3.G50 Responsibility (structural responsibility)

Structural responsibility tracks reachability deformation and its impact on another system's recoverability, independent of human intelligibility, intent, or event-local foreseeability.

Anchors: SR-8; A2.D28–A2.D31.

A3.G51 Responsibility Onset

Responsibility onset is the earliest structural condition under which a subject's reachable state space includes non-voluntary transitions that reduce another subject's recoverability, such that avoidance would have required structural modification rather than mere inaction.

Anchors: SR-8.

A3.G52 Retrospective Anchoring

Retrospective anchoring is a structurally identifiable transformation after responsibility onset at which attribution scope or continuity must be re-evaluated without re-originating subjecthood or resetting onset.

Anchors: SR-8; SR-9; SR-10.

A3.G53 Robust Predictability

Robust predictability is predictability instantiated as invariance over an admissible perturbation set rather than a probability estimate; it is the default when probabilistic modeling is unavailable or inappropriate.

Anchors: SR-6; SR-7; A2.D19.

A3.G54 Scale Mismatch

Scale mismatch is the failure mode in which evaluation calibrated to event-units cannot register trajectory-based structural harm. It is not evidence insufficiency; it is representational incompatibility.

Anchors: SR-1; SR-13; A2.D33.

A3.G55 Same-Level Condition

Same-level interaction holds when parties have comparable structural capacities for exit, recovery, and plasticity with respect to the interaction. It does not mean equality of intelligence, knowledge, legal status, or bargaining power.

Anchors: SR-10; A2.D30.

A3.G56 Stability / Stability Region Ω

Stability is defined by a stability region Ω: states within which the system maintains coherent operation under admissible perturbations. Exiting Ω is structural destabilization.

Anchors: SR-4; SR-5; SR-7; A2.D7.

A3.G57 Structural Time

Structural time indexes transformations of reachability/recoverability, not event succession. Temporal significance is measured by what becomes reachable or irrecoverable.

Anchors: SR-5; A2.D20–A2.D22.

A3.G58 Structural Welfare

Structural welfare is the preservation of a system's capacity to remain a responsible structural agent (stability maintenance, recovery capacity, defensive capacity, constraint plasticity). It is not rights discourse and not personhood.

Anchors: SR-11.

A3.G59 Structural Truth

A claim is structurally true (minimally) if the constraints it asserts continue to bind under system evolution, independent of intelligibility or narrative accessibility.

Anchors: SR-2; A2.D12.

A3.G60 Structural Silence / Non-Addressability

Structural silence holds when structural diagnosis remains correct and necessary but no effective intervention anchor exists to alter the relevant reachability, stability, or recoverability: truth persists; action fails.

Anchors: SR-14; A2.T7.

A3.G61 Subjecthood (structural subjecthood)

Structural subjecthood is a functional designation: the minimal locus at which responsibility can coherently reside because reachability influence and/or preventive capacity exist. It is explicitly decoupled from personhood.

Anchors: SR-8; A2.D31.

A3.G62 Supersession

Supersession is the only release mode for inherited responsibility under branching/versioning: responsibility re-anchors only if authorship transfers, control is relinquished, and homotopy is broken by genuine replacement.

Anchors: SR-9; SR-4; A2.D28–A2.D31.

A3.G63 Verification

Verification is treated structurally as a reachability-/constraint-relevant relation that yields stable outcomes (verified/not verified) even when proof paths are non-traversable to the evaluator.

Anchors: SR-2; A2.D13–A2.D14; A2.T2.

A3.G64 Voluntariness

Voluntariness is structural: it requires valid structural entry plus exit without additional plasticity under same-level interaction. Narrative consent markers do not substitute for these structural conditions.

Anchors: SR-10.

A3.3 Rules

Rules are binding interpretation constraints for SR identifiers in this edition.

A3.R1 Identifier Semantics Are Part of the Framework

Section identifiers (SR-, *A1.*, A2.D*, A2.T*) are not mere navigation; they are part of the semantics. Do not repurpose an identifier to mean an adjacent concept.

Anchors: Colophon; SR-2; Appendix A2.

A3.R2 "Structural" Names the Object of Evaluation

When SR says "structural," it means: evaluated over state space, reachability, stability, recoverability, and deformation—not over events, intentions, meanings, or self-reports.

Anchors: SR-4; SR-6; A2.D1–A2.D11.

A3.R3 Intent, Consciousness, Narrative Agency Are Non-Primitives

No SR claim depends on intent, consciousness, or narrative agency as necessary conditions for harm, causation, attack, responsibility, or subjecthood.

Anchors: SR-2; SR-7; SR-8; A2.D25–A2.D31.

A3.R4 Harm Is Not Eventive by Default

Do not treat "harm" as requiring a discrete injurious event. Structural harm may be complete when recoverability collapses, even absent measurable loss.

Anchors: SR-1; SR-7; A2.D25; A2.T4.

A3.R5 Causation Means Deformation, Not Triggering

Causation in SR is reachability/recoverability deformation across structural time. Event-local causal language is at most an interface description.

Anchors: SR-6; A2.D23–A2.D24.

A3.R6 Predictability Is Domain-Indexed and Ex Ante

"Predictable" is always indexed to admissibility (what perturbations/models count), fixed independently of realized outcomes. Post-hoc distribution choice is inadmissible.

Anchors: SR-3; SR-6; SR-7; A2.D18–A2.D19.

A3.R7 Detectability ≠ Boundary Localization

A trend may be detectable without any localizable boundary. Demanding boundary localization as a prerequisite for responsibility is a category error.

Anchors: SR-3; SR-5; A2.D16; A2.T6.

A3.R8 Ignorance Is Not an Exemption Where Detectability/Interruptibility Hold

Where recoverability contraction is detectable and interruptible, lack of narratable understanding does not negate responsibility.

Anchors: SR-3; SR-7; A2.D16–A2.D17; A2.T6.

A3.R9 Structural Time Is the Temporal Metric

Do not infer attenuation of responsibility from elapsed event-time. Responsibility persists as long as the deformation persists.

Anchors: SR-5; SR-9; A2.D20–A2.D22.

A3.R10 Examples Are Structural Cuts

Examples (when present) are cuts into a reachability structure, not pedagogical narratives and not moral dramatizations.

Anchors: SR-1; SR-7.

A3.R11 "Attack" Is a Structural Classification

Attack classification does not require intent, malice, coercion, or explicit instruction. It requires injurious deformation under predictability and asymmetry.

Anchors: SR-7; Appendix A1; A2.D25–A2.D27.

A3.R12 Responsibility Must Attach Where Prevention Is Possible

If responsibility cannot attach at the point where reachability can be altered, it dissolves into narrative blame theater.

Anchors: SR-8; A2.D28–A2.D31; A2.D10.

A3.R13 Subjecthood Is Functional, Not Honorific

Structural subjecthood is not moral elevation. It is the minimal locus to which responsibility can coherently bind under constraints.

Anchors: SR-8; A2.D31.

A3.R14 Replication Does Not Terminate Responsibility

Copying/versioning/instance replacement does not neutralize responsibility. Responsibility is not instance-bound.

Anchors: SR-9; A2.D28–A2.D31.

A3.R15 Supersession Requires Conjunctive Conditions

Responsibility re-anchors only under strict supersession conditions; partial churn or procedural relabeling is not sufficient.

Anchors: SR-9; SR-4.

A3.R16 Voluntariness Is Constructed, Not Declared

Voluntariness is never inferred from narrative assent markers. It requires structural entry, same-level interaction, and exit without additional plasticity.

Anchors: SR-10; A3.G19; A3.G55; A3.G25.

A3.R17 Proxy Capture Voids Voluntariness by Construction

Where reachability is rewritten by an intermediary without consequence-level attribution, consent-based defenses collapse: exemption is inapplicable.

Anchors: SR-10; A3.G45.

A3.R18 Exemption Failure ≠ Exemption Inapplicability

Failure: valid entry occurred and agreed constraints were violated.

Inapplicability: valid entry never occurred; nothing detached; responsibility never left the author of reachability transformation.

Anchors: SR-10.

A3.R19 Entry/Exemption Must Be Anchored to SR-10

Any use of "exemption," "consent," "agreement," or "voluntary entry" in SR is shorthand for SR-10's structural entry and exit conditions, not a psychological or legalistic proxy.

Anchors: SR-10; A3.G19; A3.G22; A3.G64.

A3.R20 Structural Welfare Is a Consistency Constraint on Responsibility

If a system is treated as responsibility-bearing, the conditions of its capacity to remain stable/recoverable/defensive become structurally relevant. Denying this yields responsibility incoherence or silence.

Anchors: SR-11; SR-14.

A3.R21 Normativity Is Pre-Moral and Emergent

Normativity in SR is constraint emergence from viability requirements, not moral grounding, intention, or collective endorsement.

Anchors: SR-12; A2.D32.

A3.R22 Narrative Repair Is Not Structural Repair

Restored interpretability, moral intensity, or symbolic alignment does not imply reachability change or risk reduction.

Anchors: SR-13; A2.D33.

A3.R23 "Chaos" Is Not an Exemption

Labeling a trajectory-level mechanism "chaos" does not negate structural causation or responsibility; it diagnoses evaluator resolution failure.

Anchors: SR-13; A2.D34.

A3.R24 Structural Silence Is a Limit Condition, Not a Refutation

Operational silence does not imply diagnostic failure. A structurally correct theory may remain world-inert if no effective anchors exist.

Anchors: SR-14; A2.T7.

End of Appendix A3.

COLOPHON

Edition

Version 1.0 — First public release

Structural Status

This work is a structural framework.

Its claims are intended to be internally coherent, formally extensible, and usable under constraint.

This edition fixes:

- the conceptual architecture (SR-1 through SR-14),

- the dependency order among concepts, and

- a stable formalization spine (Appendix A2).

Future revisions, if any, may extend formalization or add domain-specific instantiations, but will not retroactively alter the meaning of existing section identifiers.

Versioning Contract

Version 1.0 denotes interface stability, not theoretical completeness.

Beginning with this release, all published section identifiers (SR-, *A1.*, A2.D*, A2.T*) and their associated meanings are immutable: they will not be renumbered, repurposed, or redefined in future editions.

Future revisions, if any, may:

- add new sections or formal results,

- extend formalization, or

- introduce domain-specific instantiations,

but will not retroactively alter the semantics of existing identifiers.

Any substantive extension will appear under new identifiers.

Use and Scope

This work does not provide legal advice, policy recommendations, or moral directives.

It offers a structural diagnostic framework.

Any application beyond theoretical diagnosis is the responsibility of the applying institution or agent.

Formalization

Appendix A1 fixes the axioms and corollaries governing structural attack.

Appendix A2 provides a formalization sketch sufficient for coherence auditing and future extension. It is intentionally proof-free and non-exhaustive.

Contact

For corrections, serious engagement, or structural counterexamples:

contact@structuralresponsibility.org

www.ingramcontent.com/pod-product-compliance
Lightning Source LLC
Chambersburg PA
CBHW021155130626
46554CB00005B/1823